YORKTOWN
VIRGINIA

YORKTOWN
VIRGINIA
· A BRIEF HISTORY ·
WILFORD KALE

THE
History
PRESS

Published by The History Press
Charleston, SC
www.historypress.com

Front cover, top: Library of Congress; *bottom*: Copyright © Alexander Kravets, Alexander's
Photography, Yorktown, Virginia.
Back cover: Library of Congress; *left insert*: courtesy of Shiloh Baptist Church, Philadelphia,
Pennsylvania; *right insert*: Courtesy of the Central Rappahannock Heritage Center.

First published 2018

Manufactured in the United States

ISBN 9781467139571

Library of Congress Control Number: 2018945793

For William A. "Will" Molineux and Louise Lambert Kale

CONTENTS

CONTENTS

ACKNOWLEDGEMENTS

There is absolutely no way to research, compile and write a book of this nature without tremendous help from dozens of people. And there is no way this book could have been completed without the assistance of Will Molineux and Louise Kale. Will is a wealth of historical information. A friend of many years, he served as longtime bureau chief and newspaper editor in the Williamsburg, Yorktown, Newport News area for the *Daily Press*. He has a strong overview of the history of Yorktown, which I tapped frequently. Louise, my former wife, is a masterful copy editor and knows when I change tenses in midsentence and when I simply don't use enough commas to make something read correctly. She has worked on many of my other books. Will and Louise read the chapters, in some cases twice. Thanks to them, and this volume is dedicated to them.

Kate Jenkins, acquisitions editor at The History Press, should probably be given combat pay for her work on this volume. She guided me through this many-months effort and was marvelous! Thanks, Kate. Thanks also go to The History Press copyeditor Rick Delaney.

An essential thank-you goes to a number of special folks, including Mary Ann Williamson, a world-class copy editor and book guru. Dr. Kelley Deetz of Randolph College and Dr. Julia Ann Sweet of Baylor University allowed me to utilize their honors and master's theses, respectively. They also were most generous with their time. Jim and Ann Krikales (Nick's Seafood Pavilion), Floyd Hill Jr. (Slabtown) and Troy Griffin (Slabtown) spent much time providing valuable recollections. Francine Archer, Special Collections and Archives, Virginia State University, helped immensely in the search for several important photographs.

Anne Johnson in Special Collections at the Earl Gregg Swem Library, College of William and Mary, went out of her way to scan illustrations, many at the last minute. Thanks also go to Jay Gaidmore, director of special collections, and Kim Sims, university archivist, at the William and Mary Library. Particular thanks go to Marisa Porto, editor and publisher, and Adrian Snider and Susan Conner of the Newport News *Daily Press*.

Helpful appreciation goes to Robert Jeffrey, Jamestown-Yorktown Foundation; Gail Whittaker, York County public information officer; Jessica A. Wauhop, marketing specialist, York County Parks and Recreation & Tourism; Melanie A. Pereira, conservator, Colonial National Historical Park, National Park Service; Jennifer Carver, regent, Comte de Grasse Chapter, Daughters of the American Revolution; Quatro Hubbard, archivist, Virginia Department of Historic Resources; Kim Anderson, audiovisual materials archivist, State Archives of North Carolina; Janet T. Fast, editor, *Chesapeake Style*; Trevor A. Wrayton, senior photographer, Office of Public Affairs, Virginia Department of Transportation; and John Reifenberg, collections manager, Central Rappahannock Heritage Center.

Thanks also to Cassie L. Phillips, Shiloh Baptist Church; Kathleen Manley, Yorktown author; Richard Shisler, Yorktown postcard collector; the Reverend Edward Sparkman, pastor, Shiloh Baptist Church, Philadelphia, Pennsylvania; Bob Barker, archivist and Marc Marsocci, director of digital services, Mariners' Museum; and Steve Ormsby, president, and Michael Steen, director of education, the Watermen's Museum.

A special thank-you to my best friend, Sig Huitt of Rock Hill, South Carolina, for his constant support, encouragement and splendid proofreading.

The patience, love, care and perseverance of my wife, Kelly, along with the encouragement of my sons, Walker and Carter, and my daughter, Anne-Evan K. Williams, helped bring this project to fruition.

INTRODUCTION

Take a walk down the narrow streets of the quaint village of Yorktown with its historic and restored colonial-era buildings. Below the bluffs is a modern-day small shopping area at the water's edge with an expansive sandy beach.

It is hard to realize that in the mid-1700s this community of more than two thousand people occupied between two hundred and three hundred cottages, homes and mansions for merchants, craftsmen and tradesmen. Additionally, there was a bustling wharf with numerous warehouses and piers extending to the deepwater channel.

Back then, Yorktown was one of Virginia's major ports. However, through the years, two wars, a massive fire and a major decline in the tobacco export business led Yorktown to gradually wane.

The only surviving attribute is its history.

In the American Revolution, Yorktown was the site of the last major battle of the war. British general Charles, Lord Cornwallis, spent a portion of 1780 and 1781 fighting in the southern colonies of North and South Carolina and, finally, Virginia. By an act of fate, Lord Cornwallis found himself and his well-fitted troops at the end of the Virginia Peninsula in the early fall of 1781.

Hoping for rescue by a British fleet sent from New York, Cornwallis awaited an exit. But as it would happen, a French fleet from the West Indies arrived off the mouth of Chesapeake Bay and sent the British back north. In the end, there was nothing left for Lord Cornwallis but surrender.

The French and American troop alliance at Yorktown with George Washington and French commander Comte de Rochambeau sealed his fate. That alliance and ultimate victory has been celebrated with parades and festivities ever since. Big celebrations occurred in 1881, 1931 and 1981. Each in its own way rekindled the excitement and importance of Yorktown.

Yorktown came back on the scene briefly in 1862, when Confederate forces found themselves embattled with Union troops under the command of Major General George McClellan, who was seeking to advance up the Virginia Peninsula in an effort to capture the Confederate capital of Richmond. The encounter lasted only three or four weeks. Many of the fortifications were erected adjacent to or upon Revolutionary redoubts.

Following the Civil War, the area gradually settled back to its Revolutionary habitat. In 1930, the federal government began an effort to save the eighteenth-century community and battlefield. The Colonial National Monument (later renamed the Colonial National Historical Park) was created with headquarters here and a companion park seventeen miles away at Jamestown, the 1607 site of the first permanent English settlement in the New World. The Colonial Parkway connected these two elements; the first phase of the roadway from Yorktown to Williamsburg was completed in 1937. The final link from Williamsburg to Jamestown was completed in time for the 350th anniversary of the Jamestown settlement in 1957.

The National Park Service—Yorktown's major tenant—includes property protecting the battlefield and historic sites within the old town plat, while at Jamestown, nearly the entire island was secured. (The 1607 landing and fort site on the island is owned by Preservation Virginia, the successor to the Association for the Preservation of Virginia Antiquities [APVA].)

A number of military installations also have made Yorktown their home through the years, including the U.S. Coast Guard Reserve Training Center (site of the original port of York) and the U.S. Navy Weapons Station, which today includes adjacent Cheatham Annex.

Yorktown has embraced its history while trying to remain a viable twenty-first-century small community with enhanced tourist appeal.

1

COLONIAL PORT OF YORK

T obacco and slavery helped launch and develop the Port of York. Today, Yorktown provides no inkling as to the size and success of the colonial-era port with its vast wharfs, piers, docks and associated storehouses and taverns clustered along the waterfront just yards from the York River's major deepwater channel.

The Virginia General Assembly created an act in 1691 for the establishment of ports in the counties of the colony to provide centers for commerce and trade. Several earlier attempts to encourage development of port towns had been unsuccessful.

The failures created an ungoverned trade of tobacco that led to varied tobacco prices and eventually to the falling value of the product. The lack of port towns had "rendered impossible to be secured [the customs and revenues from trade goods that were] to be duly paid into the hands of their majesties respective collectors, and other officers thereto appointed," according to the act.

The Port of York came about within months of the act's passage, when Benjamin Read of Gloucester County, grandson of an early settler in the area, sold fifty acres for the creation of the town. Surveyor Lawrence Smith laid out eighty-five half-acre lots on the bluffs above the York River. On November 24, 1691, thirty-six lots were sold; within the next year, twenty-five more lots had owners, York County records indicate.

A strip of land, however, below the bluffs between the newly platted town and the river was declared "a Common Shore of no value." That

Yorktown viewed from the York River in 1755 by artist John Gauntlett aboard the HMS *Norwich. Courtesy of the Mariners' Museum.*

strip officially became part of Yorktown in 1738. It was called "common ground" because the town's trustees held the property for all the citizens. (The trustees, a body designated by the court in part to protect the ground, survived until 2003, when the Virginia General Assembly abolished the trustees and conveyed the property to York County.)

The Port of York story began about 1620, when Captain Nicholas Martiau, a native Frenchman, came to Virginia specifically to build a fort on the York River. That fort was intended to complete the grand log palisade across the Virginia Peninsula between College Creek off the James River and Queen Creek off the York. Martiau was the grandfather of Read, who sold the land for the town.

The fort, part of York Shire—originally Charles River Shire and later one of the original shires (counties) established in the colony in 1634—was built a short way downriver from present-day Yorktown. The original site sat on land that is now part of the U.S. Coast Guard Reserve Training Center. A small settlement grew up around the fort, because colonists felt it offered them safety.

In the mid-1600s, lush lands along the York River's south bank at plantations such as Kiskiack, Ringfield and Bellfield began to produce a sweet-scented tobacco. This tobacco became highly prized not only in Virginia but also elsewhere in the colonies and in England, where it became a top import. This tobacco variety developed over several decades in part from the seeds acquired from the West Indies by colonist John Rolfe (husband of Powhatan princess Pocahontas).

(The native Virginia tobacco, called Apooke and grown by the Indians, was *Nicotiana rustica*, which early colonist William Strachey described: "yt is not of the best kind, yt is but poore and weake, and of a byting tast" not pleasing to English smokers.)

Drawing on their success, the planters desired to produce more. With the money they were earning, they purchased the slaves and indentured servants needed to increase crop sizes. According to author Mark St. John Erickson in the Newport News *Daily Press*, the acquisition of many slaves was made possible when the Royal African Company "brought the transatlantic slave trade to Virginia in the 1670s. And then that monopoly ended in 1689—opening the trade to other English merchants—the appetite for black labor quickly transformed the York into what was for fifty years by far the biggest slave market in Virginia."

During those years, more than two hundred slave ships landed at the Port of York. The "enslaved blacks trickled down from the elite [plantations] to the middling and smaller planters of York County, too, making it the first part of the [Virginia] colony in which slavery became broadly based." By the

This woodcut depicts tobacco ships at a Virginia dock in 1661. *From the author's collection.*

An early nineteenth-century tobacco label advertising the Virginia product available at the Dagger on Bread-Street-Hill, Queen-Hith, London. *New York Public Library.*

mid-1700s, in addition to the field hands, house slaves could be found working in taverns and in homes throughout the area. It was estimated that by the beginning of the American Revolution, approximately 31,000 blacks had been sold into slavery along the York River.

From the very beginning, the port had piers that extended to the deepwater channel to allow for the loading of a variety of goods, including the aforesaid choice sweet tobacco, to be transported to England and throughout the Atlantic Ocean region. Gradually, in the early 1700s, the port emerged as a major shipping and economic center. The waterfront expanded as more planters sought to become involved in exporting tobacco and as merchants developed businesses that imported a wide variety of goods.

Within twenty years of its establishment, the port had a well-developed waterfront boasting wharves, docks, storehouses and businesses, including taverns for both drinking and lodging. On the bluff above, merchants' and craftsmen's houses as well as stately homes lined Main Street. Taverns and other shops were scattered throughout the town. By 1750, the height of Yorktown's prosperity, between 250 and 300 buildings existed in the community, and the population had grown to nearly two thousand people.

Water Street developed along the shoreline with three connecting streets—Buckner, Read and the "Great Valley"—stretching down the bluffs from Main Street to the river. Like other eighteenth-century river towns in eastern Virginia—Urbanna, Port Royal, Dumfries and Occoquan—Yorktown included persons of all types: wives, mothers and children, along with shopkeepers, merchants, planters, yeomen, indentured servants, slaves, travelers and seamen.

An unidentified English visitor in 1736 wrote:

Yorktown had a great Air of Opulence amongst the inhabitants, who have some of them built themselves Houses, equal in Magnificence to many

A detail from an early eighteenth-century engraving, *A Tobacco Plantation. Library of Congress.*

of our superb ones at St. James's.... [T]he Taverns are many here, and much frequented, and an unbounded Licentiousness seems to taint the Morals of the young Gentleman of this Place. The Court-House is the only considerable public Building, and is no unhandsome Structure.... The most considerable Houses are of Brick; some handsome ones of Wood, all built in the Modern Taste; and the lessor Sort, of Plaister.

Merchants in Yorktown began to import goods frequently destined for the stores and shops of Williamsburg, Virginia's colonial capital only twelve or so miles away. Ships from Great Britain brought the needed goods and then filled their holds with hogsheads of tobacco. The list of goods is almost endless. National Park Service historians have pointed out that "incoming freight included clothing, wines and liquor, furniture, jewelry and silver plate, riding gear and coaches, swords, firearms, books and slaves."

Yorktown was battered September 7–8, 1769, by a hurricane that many meteorology historians consider one of the worst storms of the eighteenth century. Alexander Purdie and John Dixon's *Virginia Gazette* newspaper called it "a most dreadful hurricane;" the rain "came down in torrents;" and the damage "must be inconceivable." The paper's September 21 edition reported:

> *The shipping &c at York have suffered greatly.…Capt. Banks, for Liverpool, is ashore below Wormley's Creek with 11 Feet of water in his hold and it is supposed cannot be gotten off.…Capt. Hamlin, lately arrived from London, cut away its main and mizzen masts, and was the only vessel in York that rode out the storm.…A light sloop of Captain* [John] *Whiting is sunk on Gloucester Point* [across from Yorktown].…*The top of the wharf was carried away, and drove against Mr. Jones's store, which saved that from being swept off likewise.*

Another schooner rammed its bowsprit into a storehouse, according to marine historian Arthur Pierce Middleton. Two vessels found themselves aground on "Colonel Digges's marsh" just upriver from Yorktown. One was loaded with rum; the other, "with two hogsheads of tobacco on board," was "stove to pieces."

With the coming of the American Revolution, Yorktown, like other coastal ports, suffered from a major reduction in British trade. In 1781, the town suddenly found the war on its doorstep. British troops under Charles, Lord Cornwallis, were trapped at Yorktown, where the general had hoped to be rescued by the British fleet. However, French warships at the mouth of nearby Chesapeake Bay kept the British away.

General George Washington and French commander Comte de Rochambeau and their allied forces encircled the town and laid siege. The British defenses could hold out for only so long. Ultimately, on October 19, 1781, a surrender document was signed and peace secured.

Major portions of the town, however, were destroyed or severely damaged by the French-American artillery and the inevitable ravages of war. Many residents simply abandoned their homes and shops instead of trying to repair them. Those who stayed worked for many years recovering.

What had not been ruined by the war was devastated thirty-two years later by a massive fire on March 3, 1814. Some reports stated the fire began on the waterfront, while others contended it started on top of the bluffs. The *Richmond Enquirer* published a detailed account of the disaster:

A detail from the cartouche of the Joshua Fry and Peter Jefferson map of Virginia, drawn in 1751. Hogsheads of tobacco are seen being readied for export. *Library of Virginia.*

> *Yorktown—Yesterday about 3:00 p.m. Mrs. Gibbons' house in this place took fire and together with the county Court-house, the Church, the spacious dwelling of the late President Nelson* [William Nelson, president of the colonial governor's council], *and the whole of the town below the hill, except Charlton's and Grant's houses, were consumed. The lower town was occupied principally by poor people who are now thrown upon the world without a shelter or a cent to aid them in procuring one.*

The *Enquirer* added, "The wind was high and the [buildings] were old—the fire spread, of course, like a train of powder."

Mrs. Gibbons (possibly Mary Gibbons) was the owner of a well-known tavern situated at the upper end of the town near the church off Main Street. Her establishment appeared to be where the fire started. How it started is unknown, although allegations were made against "marauding British soldiers." Throughout the War of 1812, British troops were often nearby on land or on the York River.

Attorney Robert Nelson, son of Thomas Nelson Jr., a signer of the Declaration of Independence, wrote to St. George Tucker of Williamsburg that he presumed some houses off Main Street "and those under the hill must have taken fire from the church." He also told Tucker of the loss of several Nelson family homes. "I suppose there must be between twenty and thirty houses destroyed. How the Houses on the left side of the street between the court house and my Aunt Nelson's escaped I cannot conceive." Again, many Yorktown residents found it better to leave than rebuild.

The last piece in the Yorktown destruction saga came with the Civil War. Union general George McClellan's Peninsula Campaign in the spring of 1862 was an attempt to defeat the Southerners and capture the Confederate capital of Richmond. The Confederate forces set up a defensive line around the town, just as the British had done thirty-five years earlier. The Union troops shelled the community and were prepared to extend the onslaught for weeks before the Confederates evacuated.

Confederate battery with eight-inch Columbiads on top of the cliff looking out over the York River after the April–May 1862 siege. Union soldiers are around the battery. *Library of Congress.*

Having forced the Confederates out, Union troops commandeered the town and remained until the end of the war. The most vicious blow for the town came on December 13, 1863, when the courthouse, built after the 1814 blaze, erupted in flames. Union troops had stored ammunition and powder in the building, and it exploded. According to reports, the explosions could be heard for three hours or so; fifteen neighboring structures also were destroyed.

Yorktown never really recovered from the devastation. Major structures such as the colonial-era Swan Tavern and the 1737 jail were lost; only a handful of the colonial structures remained.

2

GRACE CHURCH SURVIVED FIRE AND WARS

Battles of two wars were fought around Grace Church. Although severely damaged, it survived both encounters. In the Revolutionary War, British forces, while building and maintaining defensive fortifications around Yorktown in October 1781, used the structure to store munitions—apparently the only time it wasn't used as a church.

Eighty years later, Confederate forces, also defending the town, placed a major naval battery—with large cannon—not far from the church. Again, the building, battered and bruised, survived destruction.

The structure was built about 1697 as the York-Hampton Church, affiliated with the Church of England, the established church of the colony. It was constructed out of marl, "a lime-rich mud or mudstone that contains variable amounts of clays and silt." In fact, Virginia architecture historians believe the church "is one of the few, if not the only, surviving colonial structures built of marl." Marl is soft but hardens almost to stone when exposed to the air. The marl for the church probably came from the cliffs nearby; the walls were twenty-seven inches thick, which may explain while they survived the Revolutionary War, the Great Fire of 1814 and Civil War bombardments.

Historians believe that the present Grace Episcopal Church, located just off Main Street on the bluff above the York River, is the third parish church of York Parish, established in 1638. The first two churches, built in 1642 and 1667, were located downriver at the first Port of York settlement, now the U.S. Coast Guard Reserve Center. A tombstone dated 1655 of a William

A naval battery photograph by George N. Barnard, part of Mathew Brady's photographic team, was taken in May 1862. Grace Church, in the background, served as a hospital for Union troops. *Library of Congress.*

Gooch can be seen today on the grounds of the Coast Guard center; it is within the foundation walls, which indicate that the first two churches were built on the same site.

The construction date of Grace Church has not been pinpointed, but the county order book of November 26, 1696, notes a pledge of £20 sterling toward the construction of a brick church within the next two years. The church was built not with bricks but with the aforementioned marl. According to historian Charles E. Hatch Jr., the original church was a rectangle measuring twenty-eight by fifty-five feet with the main entrance at the west end and the altar, as usual, at the east. The building was placed angularly on Lot 35.

In 1706, York Parish was combined with Hampton Parish to form York-Hampton Parish, with Grace Church serving the new parish. With the growth of church membership, the building was expanded sometime prior to 1760, with an addition built on its north side measuring twenty-eight by twenty-nine feet. Like the original walls, it, too, was made of marl; the church became a T-shaped structure. A French billeting plan, drawn in 1781 just following the battle, also shows the expanded church with a steeple, cupola or bell tower built on top of it. A French officer on a reconnaissance mission down the York in the fall of 1781 noted that nothing of the town was visible "but a steeple, the rest of the town being hidden by the woods."

The earliest known burial here was on September 15, 1701, when Capt. Edward Nevill was laid to rest. No marker exists for his grave, but it was duly chronicled in records now at the British National Archives, formerly the British Public Record Office. Neville was "commander of his Majesties Ship, the *Lincoln*," which had been operating in the lower Chesapeake Bay when he died.

Historians note that by 1724, the York-Hampton Church was self-supporting, with the Reverend Francis Fontaine, a professor at the College of William and Mary, as its minister. Paid the princely annual sum of 20,000 pounds of sweet-scented tobacco, he served the parish for twenty-seven years.

The Reverend John Camm succeeded Fontaine as minister in 1749 and remained until 1771. Afterward, he served as William and Mary president (1772–77). Although Camm was an ardent Tory, many of his congregation were patriots and strong community leaders such as Thomas Nelson Jr., a signer of the Declaration of Independence and wartime governor. Nelson was buried in the churchyard, and sometime in the nineteenth century, the church began to be called Nelson Church. In fact, that was what it was called around the time of the Civil War.

The church suffered greatly during the Revolutionary War. Although there were days of cannon fire directed into the town from American and French batteries, some buildings remained standing. The church was damaged and "(t)he pews & windows of the church [were] all broke & destroyed," according to York County Records involving claims for losses during the British invasion. Used by Cornwallis for military purposes, the building was restored after the war and religious services resumed.

On March 3, 1814, much of the town of York was consumed by fire, and the church and many other buildings along Main Street suffered greatly. The part of the town below the cliff at the waterside also was nearly wiped out, except for one or two houses. Only the thick marl walls of the church survived—the interior and roof were totally destroyed. For thirty-five years, the church stood in ruins while the congregation held services in private homes or public buildings.

Grace Episcopal Church about 1907, shortly after the belfry had been added. *National Park Service, Colonial National Historical Park.*

Author Henry Howe visited Yorktown in 1843 to see the community sixty-two years after the Revolutionary battle. He was taken by the serenity of the area and the splendor of the York River, a full mile wide. The river, Howe wrote, "is seen stretching far away until it merges into Chesapeake Bay—an object of beauty when rolling in the morning light; its ripples sparkling in the sun, or when its broad bosom is tinged with the cloud-reflected hues of an autumnal sunset." Regarding the church, he added, "On its banks stand the ruins of the old church. Silence reigns within its walls, and the ashes of the illustrious dead repose at its base."

By the summer of 1848, the church was "rebuilt on its former site and partly on its old walls," according to Reverend Dr. Charles Minnigerode. Minnigerode came to Virginia as a language professor at William and Mary in 1842 and began his work at Yorktown as a lay minister while studying for the ministry. He was ordained to the priesthood in 1847. (Minnigerode later served as rector of St. Paul's Episcopal Church on Capitol Square in Richmond from 1856 until 1889.) The Right Reverend William Meade, the third Episcopal bishop of Virginia, consecrated and rededicated the new building on October 31, 1848, as Grace Episcopal Church.

Another author, journalist and historian, Benson J. Lossing, visited Yorktown on December 20–21, 1848, to collect material for the *Pictorial Field Book of the Revolution* he was planning to write. Lossing was told of the Great Fire of 1814 and the much-delayed efforts to reconstruct the church, which, he noted, "is now used as a place of worship." Most of Lossing's contemporary narrative describes the graves in the old adjacent burial ground. "The tombs and monuments of the Nelson family, [are] situated a few yards from the banks of the York. Nearest to the church is the grave of the first emigrant of the family, known as 'Scotch Tom.'" Although mutilated, Lossing wrote, the stone was still "highly ornamental," about four feet high, three feet wide and six feet long. The white marble monument, made in London, included sculptured angels, a trumpet, a crown and the Nelson coat of arms.

The second monument was of Scotch Tom's son William Nelson, called "President Nelson" because he was president of the Virginia Colonial Council. "It is built of brick, with a handsomely wrought and inscribed marble slab on the top. In a vault at the end of the fragment of the brick wall seen beyond the monument, rest the remains of Governor [Thomas] Nelson," William's son and a signer of the Declaration of Independence. Lossing wrote, "There is no monument above it, and nothing marks the spot but a rough stone lying among the rank grass. Around these are strewn fragments of the stone marl of the old church wall, beautifully crystalized, and indurated by exposure."

Today, the old monuments remain, along with a new gravestone that has been raised for Thomas Nelson Jr. Erected by the Page-Nelson Society of Virginia, the stone cites the general's accomplishments and concludes with "He Gave All For Liberty."

During the Civil War, Union and Confederate armies descended upon the small costal town, causing more destruction and ruining many of the eighteenth-century homes that had survived the fire. Historian Hatch said he believes the present stucco finish on the exterior of the church was added at the reconstruction and refurbished after the war.

A freestanding tower adjacent to the building apparently was constructed sometime before the Revolutionary War and the Civil War came to town. It survived the bombardment and apparently held the 1725 bell purchased for York County. There were persistent rumors, according to Hatch, "that the Federal troops erected a signal tower on the church's roof." Records indicate there was never a tower on the roof, but rather a freestanding tower adjacent. (A contemporary photograph by Mathew Brady in 1862 confirms the fact.)

There was some internal and external damage to the church during the Civil War era, but not as extensive as during the Revolution. Economic deprivation of York County and much of eastern Virginia and a reduced size of membership kept renovations from proceeding, although worship services continued there.

In the 1890s, the church had twenty-five families on the roll and was considered a "missionary post." By 1903, some renovation apparently had

A present-day view of Grace Episcopal Church. *Photo by the author.*

taken place, since the annual report states, "Condition of property, good." At that time, a belfry was placed on top of the church. By 1925, the thirty-third annual council of the Virginia Diocese reported, "The old church is in bad condition, and repairs essential to its preservation must soon be undertaken." The renovation work closed the church from January to October 1927.

Another report from January 1927 says: "Grace Church, Yorktown is now undergoing extensive repairs. The walls which were disintegrating and spreading are being strengthened and the foundations restored. A new doorway and vestibule are being placed in the front of the church. A new belfry is being built; the roof is being strengthened and repaired; Colonial Windows are being put in the church; and plans have been drawn for a new Chancel and Vestry room. It is also proposed to put in a furnace."

The *Daily Press* reported on October 25, 1927: "All in all the old church is beaming in its new aspect." The churchyard wall was later restored. Major archaeological investigations of the church and its grounds were conducted in 1947 by archaeologist J.C. Harrington, while Lynchburg architect J. Everett Fauber Jr. began research on the building's construction. Historical research on the church itself also was undertaken; unfortunately, few records were found. After all the research was conducted, the possible donor for the restoration of the church—Lettie Pate Whitehead Evans—indicated she was not able to proceed, and the project died.

In the mid-twentieth century, Grace Church grew in membership, and a large addition was built at the rear, replacing an earlier small vestry room. The addition also served for years as the "Parish House" until a new parish house of colonial design was constructed near the church grounds in 1960. This hall was expanded in 1997.

3

WILLIAM ROGERS

"The Poor Potter"

For years, he was known simply as "a Poor Potter of Yorktown," an attribution given to him by the British royal governor.

Researchers have determined the potter was William Rogers, a prosperous Yorktown merchant and brewer, not poor at all. His enterprise, a pottery factory, was probably the largest of its kind in colonial America during the 1720s and '30s.

Through a series of excavations, researchers and archaeologists have uncovered the extent of his endeavor: he operated two kilns with adjacent support areas and manufactured mugs, porringers, chafing dishes, milk pans, bowls, colanders, churns and bird bottles (clay bottles used as birdhouses).

Rogers, however, was not a potter himself. Instead, he set up the factory and employed workmen, many from England and Europe. He did, however, manage the business and support all the efforts to enhance the pottery and the workmanship of its products.

A major effort to uncover Rogers's accomplishments came in 1968, when two College of William and Mary professors, Dr. Norman F. Barka and Dr. Ben C. McCary, and a Williamsburg high school history teacher, Dean Bailey, discovered a pit loaded with old pottery ware while digging through an exposed sewer trench in Yorktown.

Earlier fragments of Rogers's pottery had been found all over Yorktown, some carrying the initials "W.R." Other pieces were apparently used to cover roads, like oyster shells. The 1968 find, however, was the first concentration of the "poor potter's" work. Most of the pieces, Barka reported, were

Archaeologist Norman Barka cleans up the large kiln of the "Poor Potter of Yorktown," found by W.A. Childrey in 1970 beneath the dirt floor of his garage. *Special Collections Research Center, Swem Library, College of William and Mary.*

defective and probably in a pit where Rogers discarded waste pottery. In total, there were about eighty whole or cracked pots. Barka and his assistants later restored about three-fourths of them.

Along with the relatively crude and utilitarian earthenware pottery, similar to pottery found elsewhere in the American colonies, stoneware pieces were also uncovered. The earthenware included a piece of decorated "slipware," an exciting find indicating that Rogers had been experimenting with a kind of pottery made only by the English at that time. "While other potters concentrated on crude earthenware, Rogers was copying and even rivaling the English in stoneware and slipware. This shows how adept he actually was at pottery-making," Barka wrote later. It is believed that Rogers had the first salt-glazed pottery in America based on English forms and techniques.

After locating the treasure trove of Rogers's pottery, there remained one missing link—a kiln, the subject of Barka's archaeology work for nearly a decade even before the remarkable discovery. But it was not Barka who found the kiln. W.A. Childrey, a Yorktown resident, was sweeping up the dirt

Above: A drawing of a large eighteenth-century pottery kiln. The man in the illustration is five feet, six inches tall. *Special Collections Research Center, Swem Library, College of William and Mary*.

Right: Anthropology professor and archaeologist Norman Barka, circa 1972, holds a porringer uncovered at the eighteenth-century pottery site. *Special Collections Research Center, Swem Library, College of William and Mary*.

floor of his garage in the winter of 1970 when his broom uncovered several tiny, shiny green spots. He dug a little and found that the protrusions were the edges of highly glazed bricks. Childrey immediately sought professional help. Barka came to the rescue. A little serious digging revealed what the professor had been looking for—a pottery kiln.

Childrey wanted to help with the new find and even offered to knock down the walls of his garage to provide more room, but the structure proved to be good protection for the site, especially in the winter. Childrey also joked that he was glad he had earlier decided against pouring a cement floor for his garage.

A smaller second kiln was discovered a year or so later. The totality of the site proved that Rogers's pottery factory "was a large operation" on two city lots with adjacent buildings and interconnecting rooms. The smaller of the kilns may have been used as an experimental facility.

Because of the local, state and national importance of the Poor Potter and his work, the National Park Service was able to purchase Childrey's land to preserve and protect it.

Historian Martha W. McCartney and researcher Edward Ayres diligently pursued Rogers, hoping to uncover biographical information that would help describe the man. In their manuscript "Yorktown's 'Poor Potter': A Man Wise Beyond Discretion," the duo says that little is known of Rogers prior to his arrival in Virginia, circa 1710, with a wife and young daughter. Ayres believes Rogers was born in London, possibly Southwark, an area known for its pottery factories. Records revealed that he shipped various goods from England to New England and Virginia from 1700 to 1710. He apparently came of age about 1707.

Soon after Rogers arrived at Yorktown, he imported an African slave, McCartney and Ayres write. On May 19, 1711, he acquired contiguous Lots 51 and 55, upon which he established a brewery and an ordinary (a tavern often with rooms to rent). Later, the kilns, workshop and a home were erected on the lots.

Exactly when the pottery was established is not known. In the 1720s, however, court

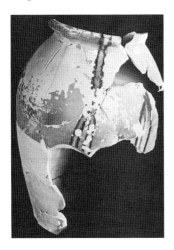

Uncovered at the pottery site was this bisque stoneware storage jar with lead glaze run. *Special Collections Research Center, Swem Library, College of William and Mary.*

records indicate that "Rogers sold quantifies of earthen wares to various plantations in Virginia, North Carolina and Maryland." By 1724, in addition to some craftsmen, Rogers had eight slaves and four white indentured servants. At his death fifteen years later, he owned thirty-six slaves.

Records show that Rogers was involved in a half dozen businesses, including grist and lumber mills, blacksmith shops, ironworks, shoe manufacturing shops and ships.

Rogers first became involved with mercantile partnerships with tradesmen in England prior to 1723. These activities necessitated his acquiring or building the storehouse or "warehouse by the waterside…under the Hill" that is mentioned in his will. From 1730 until his death in 1739, Rogers also owned at least four sailing ships, including one capable of transatlantic voyages. He bought his first ship, a ninety-ton sloop, in 1730.

Rogers also served as "Surveyor of the Landings, Streets and Cosways in York Town" and captain of a troop of horse soldiers. Gradually, he had become wealthy, joining Yorktown's "prosperous middle class," with property also in nearby Williamsburg, Virginia's colonial capital. He had risen from brewer and potter to merchant and prominent businessman.

Early in the American colonies, the royal governors generally restricted the manufacture of pottery. The economic model for the British Empire required the colonies to send raw materials to England for manufacture into finished goods. These were then shipped back for sale in the colonies. Manufacturing in America was not allowed.

Virginia lieutenant governor William Gooch was apparently well aware of Rogers's pottery efforts. In his 1732 annual report to Lords of Trade and Plantations, he dismissed a "poor potter." Gooch writes, "As to manufactures seet up, there is one poor Potter's work for course earthen ware, which is of so little Consequence, that I dare say there hath not been twenty Shillings worth less of that Commodity imported sine it was sett up than there was before." In 1739, Gooch penned, "The Poor Potter's operation is unworthy of your Lordship's notice."

In his 1745 report, Gooch explains, "The poor potter is Dead, and the Business of making potts and pans is of little advantage to his family, and is little Damage to the Trade of our Mother Country."

At Rogers's death, the pottery factory's inventory included twenty-six dozen quart mugs, sixty dozen pint mugs, eleven dozen milk pans, two dozen red saucepans, two dozen porringers, four dozen bird bottles, four dozen small dishes, three dozen lamps, four dozen small stoneware bottles, four dozen small dishes, six dozen pudding pans and thirty cream pots.

These pottery mugs were discovered during a 1968 archaeological excavation. *Special Collections Research Center, Swem Library, College of William and Mary.*

Today, the Poor Potter's kiln and the archaeological dig site are preserved and protected inside a building one block off Main Street. The 2,600-square-foot structure covers one of the kilns and a portion of his workshop. The building is situated so that visitors can walk around without exposing the historical foundations to destructive foot traffic. There is also space for interpretive exhibits about Rogers and his pottery and its impact on Yorktown. Maintained by the National Park Service, the site is open occasionally.

4
CUSTOM HOUSE DATES TO 1720s

It is not known when the two-story brick warehouse on Main Street in the middle of town became the Yorktown Custom House, but evidence indicates the building was constructed circa 1720–21.

Records show it is the oldest customhouse still in existence in the United States and also one of the oldest buildings still standing in Virginia. It is distinguished by its Flemish bond brickwork with glazed headers and by a steeply pitched hipped roof.

York County surveyor Lawrence Smith surveyed the original Port of York in 1691 with Lot 43 on the corner of Read and Main Streets where the Yorktown Custom House is located. The property was first assigned to Captain Daniel Taylor, who failed to build on the land in the allotted time, and it was forfeited. In 1706, the lot was assigned to George Burton, who paid 160 pounds of tobacco.

Ultimately, Richard Ambler, a wealthy tobacco merchant, purchased the property—Lot 43 and adjacent Lot 42—in 1720–21. The deed mentions several buildings but no brick warehouse on the land. Hence, the existing building could not date prior to 1720.

Ambler emigrated from York, England, in 1716 with his uncle Arthur Bickerdike, a merchant with connections in London. They immediately established a business in Yorktown predicated on trade between Virginia and London. Bickerdike died four years later, and Ambler took over the business and expanded his tobacco exports. Several times in the 1720s, he petitioned the Governor's Council for permission to build a storehouse and wharf on the waterfront. At this time, the Port of York was booming with the largest, deepest port between Philadelphia and Charleston, South Carolina. Ambler was one of its primary supporters.

With the large amount of trade being conducted, the English government sought to collect taxes on all the goods coming into Virginia. In 1724, Ambler was appointed collector for the Port of York River, a district that included a large area and numerous towns. With this appointment, it is quite possible that the new Main Street warehouse also became the Yorktown Custom House.

Throughout the colonies, the customhouse at major ports was a building that housed the offices that processed the paperwork related to the import and export of goods into and out of the country. Routinely, the customs agent collected a duty on all imported goods. Over the next fifty years, the Ambler family operated the customhouse, until 1776. Ambler was the customs official for thirty-five years until he relinquished the position to his

The Yorktown Custom House survived the Civil War, but the adjacent Ambler House, circa 1790, was dismantled, possibly due to war damage, not destroyed by fire as earlier believed. During the siege, it was the headquarters for Confederate major general John B. "Prince John" Magruder. *Library of Congress.*

eldest son, John Ambler, in 1759. John was the customs agent until 1766, when his brother Edward, who died two years later, succeeded him.

The third son, Jaquelin Ambler, became the collector at Yorktown in 1768 and took over the family business and properties in the port town; he also was heir to the family's political and social prominence. He continued as customs collector until 1776. During that time, he also served as a justice of the peace and York County sheriff (1771–73). He served on the Virginia Council of State from 1780 to 1782 and as treasurer of Virginia from 1782 until his death in 1798

Thomas Wyld, who purchased it from Jaquelin Ambler in about 1779, operated the building for several years as an ordinary and never returned to its customs collecting operation. During the Revolutionary War siege of Yorktown, the British used the building as a barracks; the French later did the same. Earlier, during the Ambler family occupancy of the property, a large two-story frame home was constructed adjacent to the Yorktown Custom House and connected by a covered walkway. It suffered damage during the Revolutionary War battle.

Unable to pay for the property, Wyld lost the building and adjacent home in legal action in 1783. Fourteen years later, Jaquelin Ambler sold the property to Alexander Macauley, whose family maintained ownership to the 1860s. The brick customhouse building served a variety of purposes until war returned to the town.

Confederate major general John B. "Prince John" Magruder took over the home as his headquarters in 1861–62. Earlier stories related to the building indicated that sometime during the later Union occupation, the adjacent home was destroyed by fire. An archaeological investigation in 2007, however, determined there was no fire. Instead, the house "was dismantled…although some type of damage may have led to this activity." It is believed the Ambler home "was likely scavenged by opportunistic soldiers and citizens in need of building supplies and firewood." The same fate apparently may have befallen various other buildings in town. It is possible that the Ambler house cellar was inhabited after destruction of the home.

In October 1879, a group of officials visited Yorktown in contemplation of the forthcoming centennial of the Revolutionary War surrender. A reporter for *Frank Leslie's Illustrated Newspaper* also visited and wrote: "The Custom House is a square building of the Queen Anne period, constructed of yellow brick, still yellow, but clotted here and there with white dabs. Its roof is high, the shingles moss-covered. Its windows are long and narrow,

The Yorktown Custom House, circa 1902, was owned Daniel M. Norton, a physician and politician. The Cole Digges House, circa 1730, stands at the right. Note the wagon ruts in the dirt street. *Library of Congress*.

and some of the remaining glass allows in the light of that October morning ninety-eight years ago. The original door on the south side, 'a brave bit of oak' still stands, and the cellars are now occupied by pigs."

The reporter exaggerated the influence of the Yorktown Custom House, which only handled this local Virginia region, when he wrote: "It is difficult to anchor the imagination on the fact that through this small dreary dwelling all the entries for New York, Boston, Baltimore and Philadelphia passed that this was the Custom House of this enormous continent."

After the celebration, the building sold in 1882 at public auction for $980 to Dr. Daniel M. Norton, an African American physician trained in the North who returned to Virginia after the war. Born into slavery in Williamsburg, Norton and a brother, Robert, escaped their enslavement in Gloucester County, Virginia, about 1850 and fled to Troy, New York. There, Daniel studied medicine with a local doctor and became a licensed physician. After the Civil War, both Norton brothers returned to Virginia and settled in Yorktown in late 1865.

Daniel M. Norton was a physician and politician. *Special Collections and Archives, Virginia State University.*

Daniel Norton became involved in politics and had an extensive political career for two decades. In the meantime, he put his medical office on the first floor of the Yorktown Custom House and apparently used the second floor briefly as a residence. His primary clients were African Americans who lived in a nearby community called by some "Slabtown" and later "Unionville." His successful medical practice and several other business ventures allowed him to purchase other properties throughout the area.

After only two years in Yorktown, Norton was elected to the Virginia constitutional convention—a requirement of every state that had seceded. In 1870, he lost a race for Congress, but in 1871, he was elected to the Virginia Senate. He lost his reelection bid in 1873 but regained his senate seat in 1877 and was reelected in 1879, 1881 and 1883. In 1882, he presided over the senate of Virginia for one day, April 7. At the time, the senate district encompassed the counties of Charles City, Elizabeth City, James City, Warwick, York, King William and New Kent, and the city of Williamsburg.

While serving in the senate, Norton was appointed an inspector in the Newport News Custom House and was named to the board of visitors of the Virginia Normal and Collegiate Institute (later Virginia State University). He also served as a justice of the peace in York County for many years.

In the later years of Norton's ownership of the Yorktown Custom House, his daughter taught music on the second floor, followed later by an African American school. Also in the building at one time were a barbershop, a general store and a bank.

During a portion of World War I, the customhouse again served as housing for military personnel and later for itinerant workers and their families who were working on military construction jobs nearby. The building, however, was in a sad state of disrepair.

On February 2, 1922, Emma Leake Chenoweth of Yorktown founded the Comte de Grasse chapter of the Daughters of the American Revolution; the women immediately became concerned with the deteriorating condition of the Yorktown Custom House. Later that year, Adele M. Blow, a friend of Chenoweth's, purchased the customhouse from the Norton heirs for

Founders of the Comte de Grass chapter of the Daughters of the American Revolution pose at the front door of the Yorktown Custom House. Emma Leake Chenoweth, chapter founder, is third from the right. *Courtesy of the Comte de Grass Chapter.*

$10,000. Blow was a descendent of Thomas Nelson Jr., a Declaration signer. The chapter subsequently raised money to purchase the building from Blow.

All types of fundraising projects were undertaken by the ladies to save the oldest customhouse in colonial America. Historians have described it as "a noble effort," akin to the Mount Vernon Ladies Association's efforts that saved George Washington's home and the Association for the Preservation of Virginia Antiquities' work to save the site of the Jamestown settlement.

In 1922, according to records of the Comte de Grasse chapter, there was no electricity, heat or water in the building. The fireplace still worked, and cooking was done on a woodstove. Outside window panes were missing from some windows, shutters were loose, the roof leaked and the front stoop was missing.

Renovation was desperately needed. Hopefully, restoration to its colonial appearance could be accomplished. Philanthropist Lettie Pate Whitehead Evans of Hot Springs, Virginia, a relative of another de Grasse chapter member, came to the rescue.

Richmond, Virginia architect Duncan Lee and contractor E.C. Wilkinson of Jersey City, New Jersey, were hired to head the nearly eighteen-month

A present-day view of the porch side of the customhouse with its restored gardens. *Photo by the author.*

project, which also included the reconstruction of original dependencies, a walled garden and structural restoration, both exterior and interior.

During the celebration of the bicentennial of the U.S. Customs Service in 1988, the building was rededicated, and in 1999, it was listed in the Virginia Landmarks Register. It is also included in the National Register of Historic Places.

The 2007 archaeological dig that preceded the installation of drainpipes and a dry well unveiled numerous significant artifacts. The 1861–65 military occupation of the property was emphasized by the recovery of iron cannon shot, musket and minié balls, a bayonet and Union army buttons. Fragments of numerous household items, probably from the Ambler house, were also discovered, including, buttons, straight pins, clay marbles, pieces of stoneware bottles, jugs and jars.

The Comte de Grasse DAR chapter continues to meet in the building and handles maintenance of the historic structure with funds from gift shop sales, donations and chapter dues. The chapter has developed an exhibit related to the history of the Yorktown Custom House.

5

BATTLE OF YORKTOWN

"The World Turned Upside Down"

I have the Honor to inform Congress, that a Reduction of the British Army under the Command of [Charles] Lord Cornwallis, is most happily effected," General George Washington wrote to the Continental Congress regarding the British surrender at Yorktown, Virginia, on October 19, 1781.

French general the Marquis de Lafayette, writing to a friend, put it simply: "The play, sir, is over." But it was not simple at all.

It was a great coincidence and/or an element of fate that found British lieutenant general Cornwallis, American general Washington and French general Comte de Rochambeau on the fields of Yorktown on the bluffs above the York River during that fateful fall season.

Cornwallis had decided to camp at Yorktown at what he felt was a strategic location, hoping that the British naval fleet would affect either a major supply effort or, if necessary, a rescue.

Earlier in the spring of 1781, Washington's troops were poised outside New York City while Rochambeau's French were marching through Connecticut. Washington met Rochambeau in Wethersfield, Connecticut, on May 21–22 to devise a war strategy: whether to attack New York City or move in a joint attack on the British army that was then in Virginia.

Washington favored an assault on New York because he felt the British had become weak with the movement of a large number of troops to the southern theater. The French general disagreed, feeling there were not enough troops in the combined allied forces to overcome the British scattered in the city.

Surrender of Lord Cornwallis at Yorktown is depicted on this postcard of a Nathaniel Currier lithograph after a John Trumbull painting. British soldiers walk beside Major General Benjamin Lincoln between lines of American and French soldiers. *From the collection of Richard Shisler, Yorktown, Virginia.*

Rochambeau also saw an opportunity to trap the English in Virginia and convinced Washington of his plan, especially if the French fleet in the West Indies could sail up the coast and blockade Hampton Roads.

They decided the forces would join in New York and move toward Virginia in a unified fashion, some by land and some by water, via the Chesapeake Bay.

Since March 1780, the thrust of the British military operations had been in the South, beginning with the May surrender of Charleston, South Carolina, by American major general Benjamin Lincoln, who was denied the honors of war—a set of privileges granted to the defeated army. Cornwallis, second in command under Lieutenant General Sir Henry Clinton when Charleston collapsed, assumed command of the British troops in the South immediately afterward when Clinton, commander in chief of British forces in America, returned to his headquarters in New York.

With success at Camden, South Carolina, in August, Cornwallis decided the next month to invade North Carolina. However, his subordinate, Major Patrick Ferguson, suffered a defeat on October 7 at Kings Mountain. Ferguson's loss forced Cornwallis to move his headquarters farther north from Charlotte, North Carolina, just a few miles from Kings Mountain.

The Battle of Guilford Courthouse in March 1781 was a British victory, but about one-quarter of Cornwallis's troops were killed, wounded or

Left: General George Washington. *Library of Congress*. *Right*: Comte de Rochambeau. *New York Public Library*.

missing. He then moved into Virginia in May; his aim was to achieve a decisive victory to overcome his earlier problems in his southern campaign. After spending a number of months in Virginia, Cornwallis was ordered by his superior, General Clinton in New York, to the "safe haven" on the Virginia Peninsula where he could be resupplied and receive reinforcements.

A British fleet under the command of Admiral Thomas Graves was sent from New York with the needed provisions, but fate intervened. The French fleet under the command of Admiral Comte de Grasse sailed north from the Indies and encountered the British ships off the Virginia Capes. A crucial naval battle of the Revolutionary War ensued. Twenty-four French ships of the line faced off against nineteen British ships. The French had arrived at the mouth of the Chesapeake Bay and sailed out when they saw the British on the horizon. Both sides suffered the loss of ships and men, but the British were defeated and set sail to return to New York.

Cornwallis then realized all was nearly lost.

The naval victory enabled the land siege at Yorktown. Nearly 8,000 British and Hessian troops found themselves surrounded by approximately 17,300 American and French troops—commanded by Rochambeau and Lafayette—who pounded the British fortifications around the clock with hundreds of artillery shells.

Left: General Charles, Lord Cornwallis. *Right*: Marquis de Lafayette. *New York Public Library*.

What large artillery Washington's army had been able to move from the north was dramatically enhanced when French admiral Comte de Barras's squadron was able to bring the French army's siege artillery from Rhode Island. The British simply did not have the heavy cannon to match the larger French guns.

With the British behind hastily constructed earthworks, the allied forces began to dig parallel lines. The first one was dug, primarily at night, and was completed on October 9. It was about eight hundred yards from the British; the French and American artillery had an even better opportunity to shell the town.

Within a few days, the American and French commanders decided to tighten the noose. A second parallel line was dug, again at night, to within nearly 250–300 yards of the English line. There were two remaining problems—British defenses. Before the line was completed, the outlying British Redoubts No. 9 and No. 10, close by the bluff above the river, manned by some of Cornwallis's elite troops, had to be captured. The redoubts were high earthen works surrounded by muddy ditches. Rows of abatis—tree logs with sharpened points aimed outward—provided an additional defensive shield.

A plan was devised to assault the redoubts in the night. On October 14, four hundred French troops under the command of Count William de Deux-

Colonial troops led by Lieutenant Colonel Alexander Hamilton assaulted and captured British Redoubt 10 during the Battle of Yorktown. *U.S Army Center of Military History*.

Ponts moved on Redoubt 9, and four hundred American troops commanded by Lieutenant Colonel Alexander Hamilton crept across the open space and attacked Redoubt 10.

Hamilton was not originally slated to lead the Americans. Lafayette, who commanded the American troops at that point, had selected his aide, Philippe, Chevalier de Gamit, to lead the attack. According to historian Burke Davis in *The Campaign that Won America: The Story of Yorktown*, Hamilton questioned Lafayette's decision, saying he should lead the attack. The squabble was sent all the way to Washington, who determined that Hamilton, with his seniority, should lead the assault.

The fighting involved close combat and was often heroic. Within thirty minutes, both redoubts were captured with a loss of only fifteen French and nine American troops. There was still work to be done. More trenches were dug to connect the two parallel lines, and artillery pieces were brought up closer to the British. "The increased fire," Davis writes, "stunned those still on duty in the Yorktown trenches; they had not imagined that the cannonading could become more intense." Under the day and night artillery barrage, Cornwallis made one last attempt to escape.

Lieutenant Colonel Alexander Hamilton. *New York Public Library*.

On the afternoon of October 16, the sick and wounded British soldiers were transported by rowboats across the York River to the safety of the small British fortification at Gloucester Point. Cornwallis's Council of War met, and he was persuaded that his army had to move or be destroyed. It was

British brigadier general Charles O'Hara, substituting for General Cornwallis, hands his sword to the Comte de Rochambeau in this painting by Charles Édouard Armand Dumaresq. Actually, O'Hara gave the sword to Major General Benjamin Lincoln, second in command to General George Washington. *Library of Congress.*

decided that the remaining troops would attempt, by the thousands, to cross the river in boats, break through the American and French troops there and rapidly move northward to New York.

At 11:00 p.m. that night, British regulars attempted the move, and the first boats succeeded. However, a squall swept down the river from the west as the first boats returned to pick up more soldiers, "scattering the boats and lashing the water of the narrows into whitecaps," Davis writes. A heavy rainstorm accompanied the squall; the remaining British troops on the Yorktown side did not attempt another crossing.

By midmorning on October 17, the British troops who had landed first at Gloucester Point returned to the south bank. A returning soldier reportedly told Cornwallis: "Our officers believe we will never break through there. They have trenches around our whole garrison."

The Battle of Yorktown was a success. The next day, Cornwallis sued for peace, and on October 19, the surrender was effected. Cornwallis claimed he was ill, and Major General Charles O'Hara took his place and surrendered his sword to Major General Benjamin Lincoln, Washington's second in command.

According to legend, a British band played "The World Turned Upside Down" as the British troops marched between the allied forces along a half-mile-long lane. The contrast was vivid. The French were in dress uniforms with gleaming swords and polished boots. The Americans were "clad in small jackets of white cloth, dirty and ragged, and a number of them were almost barefoot," explained eyewitness Ludwig Baron von Closen, a Bavarian on Rochambeau's staff.

When the warring ceased, Yorktown was left to pick up the pieces. Dr. James Thacher, Continental army surgeon, wrote on October 22: "I have this day visited the town of York, to witness the destructive effects of the siege. It contains about sixty houses; some of them are elegant, many of them are greatly damaged and some totally ruined, being shot through in a thousand pieces, and honey-combed, ready to crumble to pieces. Rich furniture and books were scattered over the ground, and the carcasses of men and horses, half covered with earth, exhibited a scene of ruin and horror beyond description."

6

THOMAS NELSON JR.
AND HIS HOUSE

"Aim at my house—it's the best in town," Thomas Nelson Jr. told French and American artillerymen on the afternoon of October 10, 1781. He pointed to a large two-story brick home in the middle of the town of York on the bluffs overlooking the York River.

The Battle of Yorktown that ultimately ended the American Revolution had begun the day before with some minor shelling. The real barrage, however, began in earnest on October 10, after the American units and the Grand French Battery, with its twelve twenty-four-pound and eight sixteen-pound field guns, were in place.

Some say it was George Washington who asked Brigadier General Nelson, commander of the Lower Virginia Militia, where to fire the first shot on that fateful day; others say it was the Marquis de Lafayette. Nelson singled out his own home because he suspected Lieutenant General Charles, Lord Cornwallis, the British commander, had moved his headquarters into the building.

When artillerymen proved reluctant to fire at the house, Nelson reportedly offered five guineas to the first one to hit the building. During the following week, the home was hit numerous times but not destroyed. Today, battle scars remain; two cannonballs were lodged in the brickwork in the early twentieth century on the side of the house that faced the allied artillery to show where damage used to be. After the battle, Nelson was among the American officers on the field on October 19 when Cornwallis finally surrendered, effectively ending the war.

Thomas Nelson Jr.'s house was a target during the Battle of Yorktown. This drawing by Benjamin Latrobe is from his *Essay on Landscape, Vol. 1*. *National Park Service, Colonial National Historical Park.*

Thomas Nelson Jr. was born in Yorktown in 1738. His father, William Nelson, and grandfather Thomas "Scotch Tom" Nelson were prominent business leaders of their time. (He was called Thomas Nelson Jr. because an uncle—also Thomas Nelson—was living at Yorktown during the same time. The uncle served for thirty-three years as deputy secretary for the colony of Virginia.)

Scotch Tom emigrated from Penrith, England, about 1700 and immediately developed a thriving mercantile business in the town of York. He became one of the county's leading citizens and built the Nelson house about 1730. He died in 1745.

William Nelson expanded the family enterprise by buying land and becoming a planter and a leading Tidewater tobacco merchant. William also served briefly as interim governor of Virginia (1770–71). When William died in 1772, Thomas Jr. shouldered the responsibility for the family businesses while gradually assuming a larger political role. His inheritance included an estate of twenty thousand acres, thirty thousand pounds sterling and four hundred slaves.

Thomas Jr.'s education began under the tutelage of the Reverend William Yates of Gloucester, a future president of the College of William and Mary (1761–64). In 1753, at age fourteen, Nelson traveled to England to attend Eton. He graduated from Christ's College, Cambridge, in 1761. There, he studied with a renowned scholar, the Reverend Beilby Porteus, who later became bishop of Chester and ultimately bishop of London (1787–1809).

At twenty-three years old, Nelson was first elected to the House of Burgesses from York County in 1761 while returning from England. He worked with his father in family businesses for the next decade and remained a burgess until 1774.

From the outset, Nelson actively promoted independence from Great Britain. Revolutionary tendencies mounted when the British Parliament passed a series of acts aimed at the American colonies. Subsequently, the colonial governments protested them more and more vigorously.

Thomas Nelson Jr., one of the Virginia signers of the Declaration of Independence. *New York Public Library.*

In Virginia, members of the House of Burgesses and the public learned of the Boston Tea Party and the subsequent closing of the Port of Boston. The Virginia House members, including Nelson, were determined to develop some form of action against the measure. On May 24, 1774, the leaders set June 1 for a day "of Fasting, Humiliation and Prayer, devoutly to implore the divine interposition, for averting the heavy Calamity, which threatens Destruction to our Civil Rights and the Evils of civil war."

On learning of the action, John Murray, Earl of Dunmore and British royal governor in Virginia, dissolved the assembly on May 26. The next day, "89 rebels" of the house, including Nelson, and others met at the nearby Raleigh Tavern and formed an "anti-importation association." The group also decided to call a convention of delegates from each county to meet on August 1. At that meeting, the first Virginia Convention called for all the colonies to meet regarding the growing British menace.

Nelson was quickly elected a delegate to the Virginia Conventions of 1774 and 1775. In the spring of 1775, the convention voted on a motion by Nelson to establish a Virginia militia. He was initially appointed colonel of the Second Virginia Infantry Regiment. Later in the summer, the convention appointed him to the Second Continental Congress in Philadelphia, filling the seat of George Washington, who had left to take command of the Continental army. Nelson remained a member of the Congress until May 1777.

Although Nelson was involved in various political and military activities from the mid-1760s onward, he suffered from periodic ill health, including asthma. In 1777, he was ill with a "disease of the head." This may have been the first of a series of strokes that affected the remainder of his life.

In the spring of 1776, illness forced Nelson to leave Congress briefly. While at home, he was elected a member of the "Virginia Convention" that took up the question of independence from Great Britain. Because he was also a delegate to the Congress, York County elected William Digges as an alternate to serve when Nelson was absent.

On May 15, Nelson moved a resolution drafted by Edmund Pendleton calling upon the Congress in Philadelphia to declare the United Colonies free and independent of Britain. By June 7, when Richard Henry Lee presented Virginia's resolution to the Congress that "these United Colonies are and of right ought to be free and independent states," Nelson had returned to Pennsylvania. He participated in the vigorous debate on the motion and, on July 2, voted for independence along with his Virginia colleagues—Carter Braxton, Benjamin Harrison V, Thomas Jefferson, Francis Lightfoot Lee, Richard Henry Lee and George Wythe.

During the Congress, Massachusetts delegate John Adams (later the second president of the United States) described "these gentlemen of Virginia" as "the most spirited and consistent of any" delegation. Specifically of Nelson, Adams wrote that he was "a fat man…a Speaker, and alert and lively, for his Weight." Fellow signer Benjamin Rush of Pennsylvania wrote more favorably of Nelson: "A respectable country gentleman, with excellent dispositions both in public and private life."

Most of the delegates to the Congress signed the newly engrossed (written on parchment by hand) declaration on August 2, 1776. Nelson, at age thirty-seven, became one of the founding fathers; his signature appears nine spaces directly below the large signature of John Hancock and alongside those of Benjamin Franklin and John Adams.

Between the approval of independence and the signing of the declaration, Nelson was appointed to a congressional committee on June 12 to "prepare and digest the form of confederation" for the United Colonies. By July 12, a draft of the Articles of Confederation was reported and printed secretly. Ultimately, it became the basis, after much discussion and revision, for the final document. He remained in Congress until illness forced him to resign in 1777.

In 1776, Nelson was also elected to the Virginia House of Delegates (successor to the House of Burgesses) and was reelected through 1781. He returned to the Second Continental Congress in 1779 but again became sick with violent headaches and returned home.

The Nelson House, circa 1862, on Main Street has Union army tents in the yard and is adjacent to the Sessions House (now the Shield House), one of the oldest in the town. *Library of Congress*.

The Nelson House, circa 1900, served as a hospital for Confederate and Union forces during the Civil War. *Library of Congress*.

Nelson's military service often paralleled his political life. As the Revolution continued, fear grew of a British invasion, and Nelson accepted the appointment from the government "Council" as brigadier general on August 19, 1777. The *Virginia Gazette* praised the selection of a "gentleman so universally beloved and esteemed." Several thousand militiamen were called to repel the threat, and Nelson worked hard to prepare his troops. However, after a number of weeks, he realized there was no threat and stepped down from command.

In the spring of 1778, at his own expense, Nelson formed a troop of light cavalry to aid General Washington in Philadelphia. He led the group northward but upon arrival learned they were not needed; the men returned to Virginia. All the while, he was a member of the Virginia House of Delegates.

In May 1779, Nelson found himself organizing soldiers on the Virginia Peninsula to thwart another anticipated British menace. Once more, the British did not launch a major attack. In 1780, Nelson again raised money for the American cause and personally loaned funds to the Virginia government.

In February 1781, the British finally established themselves in Virginia from Richmond eastward into the Tidewater. Nelson took command of the militia south of the James River, but an illness prevented him from taking charge. On June 4, the Virginia legislature, having moved from Richmond to Charlottesville, was almost captured along with Governor Jefferson. They luckily escaped when patriot Jack Jouett rode about forty miles from Louisa County to Charlottesville during the night to warn them.

About the same time, Jefferson notified the assembly that he would not stand for reelection as governor. Feeling that a military man would be preferred for the governorship, the body elected Nelson. Although he served only briefly, Governor Nelson was on the battlefield at Yorktown with Washington and their French allies to accept the British surrender. After he resigned, his enemies charged that he had acted during his governorship in an illegal manner by participating in this ceremony without the consent of the Council of State. Ultimately, the House of Delegates rejected the claims and resolved that Nelson's actions were entirely appropriate considering the nature of the times.

Illness overtook Nelson again, and he did not return to public service. Having lost his fortune and most of his plantations, he retired to a small property he held in Hanover County and died, very much in debt, on January 4, 1789, at age fifty.

A fine example of early Georgian architecture, the two-story Nelson House is of brick, and the corners are quoined in stone. *Courtesy of the York County Office of Public Information.*

Members of the family owned the Thomas Nelson House in Yorktown until 1914, when Captain George Preston Blow and his wife, Adele, bought it, enlarged it and called it "York Hall." The National Park Service purchased the property in 1968 as part of the Colonial National Historical Park.

The Blow additions were removed and the property restored to its eighteenth-century appearance. It is described by the park service: "Most of the Nelson House is original, including the bricks and most of the mortar in the outer walls. Inside the house, the wall panels and most of the wooden floors are original, a notable exception being the floor in the downstairs hall. The paint on the walls matches the color of the first paint applied after the house was constructed. The furnishings in the house today include reproductions and a few period pieces, none of which belonged to the Nelsons."

7

SURRENDER TERMS DECIDED AT THE MOORE HOUSE

General Charles, Lord Cornwallis, ordered a drummer at 10:00 a.m. on October 17, 1781, to beat a "parley," and a well-dressed British officer mounted a parapet south of Yorktown carrying a white flag of truce.

Within minutes, the incessant artillery barrage from the American and French cannons ceased. Lord Cornwallis then sent General George Washington a message: "Sir, I propose a cessation of hostilities for twenty-four hours, and that two officers may be appointed by each side, to meet at Mr. Moore's house, to settle terms for the surrender of the posts of York and Gloucester."

Situated downriver from Yorktown and the battlefield and outside of the combat area, the house was the residence of Augustine Moore, a local merchant and owner of several outlying plantations. Cornwallis never explained his selection of the home, and Natural Park Service officials only speculate that the building was not damaged, was a neutral site and was a convenient location for both sides.

Historians point out that Washington rejected the twenty-four-hour truce and agreed only to a two-hour cessation. However, messages were exchanged for most of the day; finally, it was determined that a meeting would be held in the afternoon on October 18. The American representative to arrange the details for the surrender was Lieutenant Colonel John Laurens of South Carolina, Washington's aide-de-camp; the French officer was Second Colonel Louis-Marie, Viscount de Noailles, the brother-in-law of

And the Guns Fell Silent is a conjectural drawing of the British call for a parley on October 17, 1781. *Courtesy of David R. Wagner, artist/illustrator.*

the Marquis de Lafayette. British representatives were Lieutenant Colonel Thomas Dundas (later a major general) and Major Alexander Ross (later a lieutenant general).

The quartet began their meeting at the Moore House in the midafternoon, but it was not until nearly midnight that final agreements were reached on the fourteen Articles of Capitulation. The room where they met is now called the "Surrender Room."

Author-historian Burke Davis explains: "The four officers haggled over every article....Ross and Laurens argued hotly that question of American deserters now in British uniform and though Laurens finally agreed to leave the article protecting the Loyalists in the agreement, he warned the British that Washington would not approve." Also part of the agreement was that the British forces "march out their troops with furled flags and with their band playing one of their own marches," Davis relates. Traditionally, the defeated were allowed "honors of war," with troops marching out with regimental flags flying and the bands playing a tune of the victors.

Laurens of South Carolina apparently remembered that at the capture of Charleston, South Carolina, in May 1780, the American army was offered no "honors of war." So, the British should suffer the same fate.

Historical records indicated that Washington reviewed the document and, as Laurens had surmised, declined to accept immunity for Tories and deserters. Cornwallis was notified of the changes, and the document was redrafted and sent back to the British. The signing took place about 11:00 a.m. the next morning, as Washington had required. There was no ceremony, but one line was added to the end of the document: "Done in the trenches before Yorktown in Virginia, October 19, 1781." At 2:00 p.m., the British troops marched out, and one of the legends has it that the band played on old English ballad, "The World Turned Upside Down." Honestly, no one knows for sure what tune was played.

The earliest published view of the Moore House. *Historic Collections of Virginia (1849).*

The Moore House was built about 1725 by Lawrence Smith II on a piece of land known as Temple Farm, which included a dam and a gristmill. The Smith family held the parcel until 1768, when Lawrence's son Robert conveyed the home and five hundred acres to Augustine Moore, the husband of his sister Lucy.

"Mr. Moore," at age fourteen, began his career as a merchant apprentice to William Nelson of Yorktown and served the company for many years. Later, in 1773, records show he was a partner of "Thos Nelson, Jr. & Co." By that time, he had inherited three plantations from his father and had become a wealthy businessman and landowner. Some believe that the family, with heritage in England, descended from the English philosopher and statesman Sir Thomas More.

Following the Revolution, the Moore family retained the home until 1797, when it was sold to Hugh Nelson, a son of Thomas Nelson Jr., a Declaration of Independence signer. The house changed hands a number of times prior to the Civil War. Unfortunately, the war wreaked havoc on the home. It was well outside the Confederate lines prior to their withdrawal on May 4, 1862. Subsequently, Federal forces were not so kind. Historian Clyde F. Trudell in his seminal book *Colonial Yorktown* charges, "During the Northern occupation much of the original structure fed the soldiers' bivouac fires." The doors, window sashes, shutters, fences and many of the weatherboards were torn out and fed to the flames.

After the war, the Moore House, as further described by Trudell, "fell into that melancholy state of desolate emptiness so typical of many fine examples of colonial architecture in Virginia ravaged by the war." He said the house served for a while as a cow barn and was occasionally occupied by transient African American farmers.

In 1879, when plans were begun for the 1881 centennial celebration of the Battle of Yorktown, a group of officials visited Yorktown; a reporter for *Frank Leslie's Illustrated Newspaper* accompanied them. The unidentified writer penned in the paper's November 1, 1879 edition that Henry Halstead, owner of Temple Farm on which the Moore House stood, allowed them to visit "his historical mansion." The shingles on the roof "are coated with the green velvet of moss." And the "Moore House is used as a store for Mr. Halstead's agricultural implements, but he assured me that it is his intention to 'fix it up' for the great commemoration of 1881."

Locally, the Yorktown Centennial Association, a joint stock company, was established to secure needed funds for the centennial festivities. The association decided to purchase Temple Farm and derelict Moore House in

Left: The ravages of war are evident in this 1862 image of the Moore House. *Library of Congress*.

Below: The Moore House prior to its 1931 restoration. The wing was added sometime early in the nineteenth century. *Library of Congress*.

order to save it for the celebration. According to the association's original plans, the house was to be a museum and lodgings for foreign guests and the farm was to be used for a military camp. Ultimately, the home was repaired, but on the celebration's first day—October 13, 1881—it "was only open to last minute workmen." The home finally opened on Sunday, October 16.

According to a master's thesis by Julie Ann Sweet of the University of Richmond (now professor of history at Baylor University), the *Norfolk Landmark* newspaper stated that Moore House "looked wonderful with its

The Moore House today with its manicured front lawn. *Courtesy of Paul Zeller, Wauchula, Florida.*

new paint and wallpaper," while the *Richmond State* said it had "an air of elegance thanks to the renovation, modern furnishings and décor from Tiffany's." However, *Harper's Weekly* lamented the changes, which "robbed [the house] of the beauty and dignity of age by the hands of vandals who had dared desecrate it and modernize it." Apparently, the *Harper's* writer had not seen the decrepit house prior to the repairs.

Sweet related that the home became "a modern country villa with fresh coats of red, yellow and green paint. Wallpaper laminated the interior walls, new carpet covered the floors, and modern furniture and trinkets advertising the dealers who sold them filled the various rooms. No museum was put into the building, but it did house dignitaries during the festivities."

Ultimately, the National Park Service purchased the house in 1931 and restored it to its colonial appearance using historic images and archaeology in the restoration, one of the first of its kind undertaken by the park service. The Moore House was formally dedicated on October 18–19, 1934, the 153rd anniversary of the surrender of Lord Cornwallis's British army.

Today, the Moore House is available to visitors on an almost daily basis under the auspices of the Colonial National Historical Park.

8

CORNWALLIS'S SUNKEN SHIPS FOUND

For about two centuries, fishermen working the York River between Yorktown and Gloucester Point brought to the surface small artifacts entangled in their nets. The objects—some of value—were from the British vessels sunk during the siege of Yorktown in October 1781.

As the American and French soldiers tightened their circle around the British troops, General Charles, Lord Cornwallis, faced numerous related decisions. Cannon fire destroyed several ships that were part of the small fleet anchored off the York shoreline. Ultimately, Cornwallis ordered the remainder of the vessels scuttled to keep them from falling into enemy hands.

Today, it has been estimated that more than forty ships, many covered with several feet of silt and oyster shells, could lie on the bottom of the York River. Thus far, ten ships have been found.

Various salvage operations have been undertaken to locate and/or explore the wrecks. On May 1, 1852, the Virginia General Assembly passed an act authorizing Thomas Ash of Gloucester County "to search for and recover the guns and any property which may have been sunk with an English frigate at Yorktown, and relinquishing the Commonwealth's right thereto." Ash had ten years of exclusivity of the rights.

Identified in the request "to fish" the wreck was the description of the ship as an "English frigate of large class," most probably the forty-four-gun frigate HMS *Charo*n, the largest warship present at Yorktown and believed to be Cornwallis's flagship. It was one of the battle's first causalities.

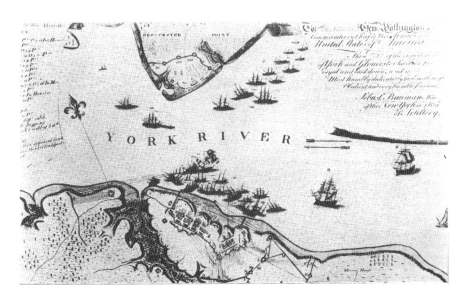

A detail from the map of the siege of Yorktown by Major Sebastn Bauman, New York Second Artillery Regiment, showing Cornwallis's fleet of ships. *Library of Congress.*

During the night of October 10, 1781, a bombardment by French artillery hit the *Charon* with "red hot shot"—cannonballs heated red hot before firing. Several struck the ship and set her ablaze; she drifted toward the Gloucester side of the river and rammed several merchant vessels. All were set afire. The *Charon* burned to the waterline and sank with a heavy loss of life. Ebenezer Denny of Pennsylvania, a major in the Continental army, wrote in his diary that the scene "was grand" and "exhibited a brilliant spectacle."

Dr. James Thacher, an American army surgeon with Alexander Scammell's Regiment of Light Infantry, who saw the bombardment from shore, wrote in his journal: "I had a fine view of this splendid conflagration. The ships were enwrapped in a torrent of fire...while all around was thunder and lightning from our numerous cannon and mortars, and in the darkness of night, presented one of the most sublime and magnificent spectacles which can be imagined."

Shortly afterward, Cornwallis ordered the remaining British ships scuttled to prevent capture and possibly to inhibit French forces from attempting an amphibious assault at Yorktown.

Ash was primarily interested in trying to recover some of the brass cannon believed to have been aboard the *Charon*. Historians later determined that Cornwallis directed the removal of most of the guns before the battle. In his

British cannon is hoisted aboard after being found in 1934–35 in the wreckage of a British ship off the Yorktown shoreline. *National Park Service, Colonial National Historical Park.*

petition to the general assembly, Ash acknowledged, "on several occasions [he] fished up from it [the wreck] some articles of value."

Francis Bannerman VI of New York City was a surplus military goods dealer in the late nineteenth century who amassed tens of thousands of items. For example, in 1870, he bought more than 200,000 surplus Springfield muskets. In January 1933, well after his death, Francis Bannerman Sons published a catalogue of military items, including a cannon from Yorktown. The catalogue claimed a diver retrieved the cannon about 1881 at the time of the battle's centennial celebration.

Artifacts continued to be recovered in the waters off Yorktown, where in the summer of 1934 a dragging effort plotted sites where potential wrecks might be located. About the same time, officials of the Colonial National Historical Park and the Mariners' Museum of Newport News agreed to conduct a salvage operation. Ultimately, the rescue efforts were centralized on a large barge moored in about forty feet of water under which wrecks were situated near the Yorktown shore. During a six-month period in 1934 and early 1935, a host of items were recovered, including three six-pounder iron cannons, three four-pounder iron cannons, several cannonballs of various sizes, pieces of gun mounts and dozens of pieces of ship's gear and equipment.

Fragments of rope and pottery were well preserved, along with numerous rum bottles. Wooden items buried below the mud were protected from the ravages of worms. Preservation efforts were far from today's sophisticated,

A four-pound naval cannon recovered from a British vessel sunk during the siege of Yorktown in October 1781. The carriage is a reconstructed piece. *Courtesy of York County.*

A string of bottles is recovered from the York River bottom during an underwater archaeological investigation in 1934–35. *Courtesy of the Mariners' Museum.*

scientific measures, and many of the iron cannons deteriorated badly within a few months of recovery. Nevertheless, the Mariners' Museum and National Park Service "were well satisfied with the results of their jointly conducted salvage operations," according to a contemporary report.

Watermen and sports divers continued to loot the wrecks, and in 1973, the Yorktown Shipwrecks were added to the National Register of Historic Places, one of the first underwater sites to be so recognized. The designation, however, did not stop the looting. Two years later, in 1975, a preliminary underwater archaeological survey was conducted at a specific site from which recreational divers were systematically removing artifacts. A year later, a field school sponsored by the Virginia Research Center for Archaeology, Virginia Historic Landmarks Commission (now the Virginia Department of Historic Resources) documented the wreck—a large merchant vessel with a cargo of British war materials.

A grant from the National Endowment for the Humanities in 1978 enabled a comprehensive survey of the York River between Yorktown and Gloucester Point. Nine wrecks were found, all British ships sunk during the Yorktown siege. Two wrecks were identified near the point. "Seven wrecks lie near the Yorktown shoreline, six of them parallel to shore as if they were part of the 'sinking line' depicted in contemporary maps," according to John D. Broadwater's account in *Archaeology in America: An Encyclopedia.*

Funds from the Virginia General Assembly and private sources enabled the creation of the Yorktown Shipwreck Archaeological Project (1978–90). In due course, the project focused on the best-preserved wreck, designated as 44Y088 and finally determined to be the collier brig *Betsy*, initially used to haul coal from Whitehaven to Dublin before it was leased by the British as a transport. Lloyd's Registry of Shipping indicates that the *Betsy* was a 180-ton vessel whose captain and owner was John Younghusband of Whitehaven, a coastal Cumbria, England community with a shipyard, where the ship may have been built. Researchers believe that since Whitehaven was heavily engaged in the tobacco trade about the time of the American Revolution, it is quite possible that the *Betsy* was in Virginia waters before the war.

"[The] small wooden ship, approximately 23 meters in length at the waterline, with a distinctly box-like shape…[with] a hull approximately 50 percent intact [contains] an interesting variety of naval and military items as well as furniture, furnishings, and personal possessions," Broadwater writes. To enable a thorough examination of the vessel in the York River's murky water with its strong currents, a steel cofferdam was constructed over the *Betsy* in 1982 and a pier built from the shore that allowed visitors to see the underwater work. The cofferdam, which encased the wreck for eight years, provided an ideal working environment for significant archaeological work on the ship's hull. The most important thing to come from the site, Broadwater said, "is the hull itself; not the many artifacts that have been found. From the hull, we've learned…about the common, everyday English merchant ship."

Underwater photograph of diver, circa 1985, examining a portion of the brig *Besty* located within a cofferdam in the York River. *Courtesy of the Virginia Department of Historic Resources.*

The underwater project ended in 1990, when the Virginia General Assembly stopped the funding, ostensibly because of a state budget shortfall. Private resources and grants later enabled the writing and publishing in 1995 of a report that includes an analysis of the effort.

In August 2010, archaeologists again pursued information on the wrecks and found a previously undetected wreck of a ship (the tenth found) that probably was scuttled by the British. According to David Hazzard, one of the divers and an archaeologist for the Virginia Department of Historic Resources, a nearly fully buried forty-foot hull section was located on the bottom of the York River in a depth of sixteen to twenty feet. It was finally determined that the ship was sixty-seven feet long and twenty-two feet wide, suggesting a vessel of about 160 tons, Hazzard added.

Underwater investigative efforts continue in the York River. Another search of a site took place in August 2013. Hazzard, who was also involved with this work, along with Broadwater and Gordon Watts, experienced underwater archaeologists, said diving work will be accomplished whenever new wrecks are found or new artifacts recovered.

Still another underwater investigation occurred in April 2018 in the York River. Organized by JRS Explorations, Inc., a Yorktown-based group, an improved high-resolution sonar was used to survey more than thirty sites between Yorktown and the Gloucester shore. It is possible that new wrecks have been found, since only ten of the known forty-some wrecks sent to the bottom have been located. The goal now is to have divers search and identify more wrecks.

9

WHAT IS THE CORNWALLIS CAVE?

Along the shore of the York River, the Cornwallis Cave is tucked into a natural marl cliff that rises just yards from the waterline. Probably dating from early colonial settlement years, the cave today can be seen only through a locked, iron-gated doorway.

Its name comes from the fact that British general Charles, Lord Cornwallis, and his troops were caught here at Yorktown during the siege of October 1781. Since the village suffered artillery bombardments frequently during the campaign, it has been suggested that Cornwallis might have sought refuge within the grotto. Probably, the cave, virtually below the town itself, was the location for military staff conferences held later in the siege. A report suggests the cave was a storehouse for wine, belonging to the "commissariat department" of Cornwallis's army.

How was the cave developed? One theory says that it was created when the bluff became the site of a marl quarry in early colonial days. Others state that there was a smaller natural opening there that was expanded, also during colonial days, for storage along the waterfront. In the mid-eighteenth century, records say specifically that potatoes were stored in the cave.

Historian Charles Campbell, who visited the ruins of the Yorktown battlefield in 1837, wrote in the *Southern Literary Messenger*: "There is a cave in the solid mass of stone marl on the riverside....I entered this wonderful cavern; but alas! There is but one step from the sublime to the ridiculous—Cornwallis's Cave is converted into a hog-pen!"

Today, the Cornwallis Cave is mostly covered by ivy with a locked, iron gate blocking access. *Photo by the author.*

Edmund Ruffin, editor of *The Farmers' Register* and acclaimed agriculture expert, visited the cave a year later. "When I entered Cornwallis' Cave," he wrote, "one of the apartments was nearly filled with fodder, and the other was converted to a hog-sty, which, in the darkness, I could not know by sight, but was soon informed by the grunting and the stench, of the presence of the successor of Lord Cornwallis." During a childhood visit, Ruffin added, the doorway was "of small size" and there were two rooms. "The walls and ceilings were shaped well and neatly; and the firmness of both showed that the excavation might be continued safely, to any extent, without any other props than walls of the marl itself." He suggested the marl could be excavated for sale.

Author Henry Howe wrote in 1845 that the cave was still "a piggery."

Benson John Lossing in his *Pictorial Field-Book of the Revolution*, published in 1855, says that he was given a tour of Yorktown in 1848 by William Nelson, grandson of Thomas Nelson Jr., one of the Virginia signers of the Declaration of Independence. Regarding the cave, he writes:

> *We first descended the river bank and visited the excavation in the marl bluff, known as Cornwallis's Cave. It is square, twelve by eighteen feet*

in size, with a narrow passage leading to a smaller circular excavation on one side. It is most directly beneath the termination of the trench and breastworks of the British fortifications, which are yet very prominent upon the bank above. Taking advantage of this tradition [Cornwallis possibly using the cave], *cupidity has placed a door at the entrance, secured it by lock and key, and demands a Virginia nine pence (12 ½ cents) entrance fee for the curious. I paid the penalty of curiosity.*

With the coming of the Civil War, the Confederate Army of the Peninsula under Brigadier General John B. "Prince John" Magruder used the cave for ammunition storage, and it became an important center of activity during the Union army's siege in April 1862.

Margaret P. Smith, historian of the local Comte de Grasse chapter of the Daughters of the American Revolution, in her 1920 book *Old Yorktown and its History*, attempts to recapture the look of the cave when a fortress, for protection, was built around it: "A passage way was constructed which led to the cave and the holes which were cut in the cave were made to hold the large beam used in making the passageway. Some time after the war

A postcard view of the Cornwallis Cave, circa 1907. *From the collection of Richard Shisler, Yorktown, Virginia.*

all of this gave way and fell in. The owner of the place cleared away the debris, dug out the place of entrance, put up a door and at the time of the Centennial of 1881 began to charge an admission fee of ten cents."

Private Oscar M. Thayer, 148th New York Regiment, Company G, on garrison duty, writes in the June 1874 issue of *Neighbor's Home Mail* magazine about a visit on February 4, 1864, to Cornwallis Cave. Thayer says there were about three hundred citizens in Yorktown when the Civil War began, but few citizens "are to be found who were here during the time the rebel force held this place....The fort [that surrounded the town] contains some 200 acres and is one of the most formidable structures of modern time." Thayer also writes: "Here it is Cornwallis had his cave....Many a curious story is told relative to this cave. We are told that no one dares to enter it, that it was inhabited by some supernatural being or spirits of men who have perished therein. After hearing these stories and many others I have resolved to visit the cave and abide the result."

Thayer and some fellow soldiers wanted to go into the cave so "we employed as guide an old Negro...[who] assured us that he had visited the cave many a time during the Revolutionary war and was familiar with all its departments. 'But,' he said, 'that was a long time ago, since that time no one dares to enter it.'"

> *We soon came to the entrance of the cave, where each one was provided with a lighted candle....We followed through a long subterranean passage seeming a quarter of a mile in length, we came out into...a large room arched overhead with brick. Here we found the old table used by Cornwallis.... From this department we descended a winding stairs, at the bottom of which found ourselves surrounded by massive walls of rocks which seemed ready to fall on us...we were told we were below the river a great ways.*

Examining this narrative, it is extremely difficult to determine whether Thayer is describing the marl cave or the surviving Confederate fort and adjacent breastworks and tunnels or interweaving all the elements. It is obvious that there was an elaborate complex involving the Cornwallis Cave.

As Private Thayer alludes to in his narrative, visitors and townspeople have heard "foreboding sounds," described as men talking and whispering, as well as groans or "incantations" coming from the cave, according to L.B. "Bob" Taylor Jr., well-known author of numerous Virginia ghost books. Taylor suggests that the voices could be "spirits of long-dead British soldiers who sought shelter" in the cave.

A Union sentry, circa 1862, is posted outside the entrance to the Cornwallis Cave. Photo by Mathew Brady. *Library of Congress.*

Sailors pay to enter the Cornwallis Cave in this 1917 postcard illustration. *From the collection of Richard Shisler, Yorktown, Virginia.*

Taylor relates that years before the cave was gated, "it was said that a group of 'devil worshipers' used the place to hold satanic rituals. Many feel that is a plausible answer to the incantations heard there." They are afraid there is evil in there.

The cave apparently has gone through a number of permeations over the years and now is not open to visitors.

10

LAFAYETTE RETURNS IN 1824

Marie-Joseph Paul Yves Roch Gilbert du Motier, Marquis de Lafayette, was a youthful, twenty-year-old French military officer who came to America in 1777, volunteering to join George Washington in the American Revolution. In American history, he is frequently referred to simply as Lafayette.

By October 1781, the handsome, young-looking Lafayette had led American forces in several skirmishes on the Virginia Peninsula and was with Washington and French compatriots who fought and defeated the British forces under Charles, Lord Cornwallis. He courageously led four hundred men who captured British Redoubt 9 on the October 14 night that Alexander Hamilton led another force against Redoubt 10.

After the war, Lafayette returned to France and was proclaimed a hero. He remained in the French army and was promoted to *maréchal de camp* over many other officers. Returning briefly to the United States in 1784, he spoke before the Virginia House of Delegates, proclaiming "liberty of all mankind," including emancipation of slaves. Prior to the French Revolution, he was commander of the French National Guard but ultimately was able to survive the revolution and the French war with Austria, after which he withdrew from politics.

On the invitation of President James Monroe, Lafayette decided to return to America in 1824–25 for a "Victory Tour." His trip to Yorktown in October 1824 was to participate in the forty-third anniversary of the battle. By the time of his visit, Lafayette was sixty-seven, stout and ailing.

After visiting Washington's tomb at Mount Vernon, Lafayette traveled on October 18 by the steamship *Petersburg* down the Potomac River and the Chesapeake Bay to the mouth of the York River. There, the *Petersburg* and an accompanying vessel were met by a five-ship flotilla that escorted them to a Yorktown wharf specially constructed for his visit.

An estimated fifteen thousand people were on hand for his welcome, including Virginia governor James Pleasants and his council and a group of army officers. Also present was John C. Calhoun of South Carolina, U.S. secretary of war.

Auguste Levasseur, Lafayette's private secretary, wrote a journal about the two-year visit and noted that Yorktown had "never recovered from the disasters" of the Revolution. Levasseur apparently was not aware of the devastating fire of 1814. "Some houses in ruin, blackened

An elderly Marquis de Lafayette visited Yorktown in October 1824. *New York Public Library.*

by fires, or riddled with bullets; the land covered with remnants of arms, bomb blasts and overturned gun carriages," Levasseur explained. He also added that tents were placed on the fields and "small squads of soldiers placed at different points," apparently as part of the pending celebration. That night, Lafayette slept in a home where Cornwallis had had his headquarters during the siege.

On the morning of October 19, Lafayette and his party went to a large campaign tent—used by Washington during the battle—that had been preserved by local citizens. There was an exchange of speeches, and Levasseur reported, "Two old Revolutionary soldiers fell down in a faint while squeezing the hand of their former general." Particular attention was paid to Colonel William I. Lewis of Campbell County, who at age fifteen led a rifle company at Yorktown. Lewis, representing "the sons of the mountains" and wearing "the mountain dress," pleaded with Lafayette to "stay with us…we will with filial affection rock with gentleness the cradle of your declining years."

About 11:00 a.m., the troops formed columns and accompanied Lafayette to a large forty-five-foot "triumphal arch" erected near the site of Redoubt 9 on the battlefield. There, Virginia general Robert Barraud Taylor, a hero of the War of 1812, made an elaborate speech and afterward placed a wreath of laurel, oak and fresh cypress on Lafayette's head. Following the battlefield ceremony, the troops marched in review for Lafayette, and the party returned to town. Elsewhere on the battlefield, a seventy-six-foot obelisk was raised at the site of Redoubt 10 and another similar obelisk was placed at the site of the British surrender. Among the officers on the field was sixty-nine-year-old Captain John Marshall, chief justice of the United States, representing the Eleventh Virginia Regiment.

While on the field, Lafayette apparently saw a familiar face and embraced him. It was James Armistead Lafayette, "a very venerable and respectable free black man," as described by the *Richmond Examiner*. During the Revolution, James, a body servant to a William Armistead of New Kent County, became a spy and reported British activities to Lafayette. At the close of the war, Lafayette gave James a certificate testifying to his Revolutionary War service. That certificate was used in James's later appeal to the Virginia legislature for his freedom.

Before the Yorktown event, the *Richmond Compiler* interviewed James Lafayette, who "expressed a great desire to see the Marquis at the approaching festival in Yorktown." He indicated, however, that he would need financial help "to equip himself [with new clothes] for the occasion." Some historians are not convinced that the former slave visited Yorktown. Nevertheless, they acknowledge that the marquis and James did meet during a parade while the Frenchman was visiting Richmond several days later. Along the route, the men recognized each other; the procession was halted as they embraced, according to the *Richmond Enquirer*.

Lafayette's secretary relayed details of Yorktown and posted interesting aspects that later were brought to Lafayette's attention. In preparation for the festivities, local residents checked numerous cellars as possible storage sites for refreshments and found a large box in the corner of one basement. "They opened it and to their great astonishment found it filled with candles, blackened by the time," Levasseur wrote. The inscription on the lid of the box showed the finders that it was part of Cornwallis's provisions during the siege.

On the night of October 19, festivities were held, including an elaborate dance. "The candles were lit that evening and placed in a circle around the camp, where the ladies came to dance the entire evening with the

James Armistead (*right*), trusted spy for Lafayette, holds his horse's bridle in a portrait portraying the Yorktown battle. Armistead added the last name *Lafayette* in honor of his friend. *Library of Congress.*

This ramshackle house served as home for Lafayette near Yorktown in 1781. This painting shows the building in May 1862 with a large military encampment during the Civil War. *Library of Congress.*

militiamen," Levasseur described. "A ball in Yorktown in 1824, by the light of Cornwallis's candles appeared so pleasant an occurrence to our old revolutionary soldiers, that notwithstanding their great age and the fatigues of the day, most of them were unwilling to retire until the candles were entirely consumed."

Lafayette and his party left Yorktown on the morning of October 20, 1824, for the next stop on his journey—Williamsburg—and a visit to the College of William and Mary, where his troops had camped in September 1781, prior to the ultimate battle in Yorktown. An elaborate men's banquet also was held at the Raleigh Tavern.

11

UNION AND CONFEDERATES IN 1862 SIEGE

A t Yorktown in early April 1862, it was a simple case of Yankee officers being outfoxed by the Confederate army into thinking the Southerners maintained thousands more men defending the town than were really there.

Confederate major general John B. "Prince John" Magruder commanded a relatively small army of fewer than 13,000 men, compared with Union major general George B. McClellan's nearly 70,000-man force that was increasing in size daily. The object, of course, was to delay the Federals until more Confederate troops could be secured. In fact, Confederate general Joseph E. Johnston's army of 25,000 would reinforce Yorktown by midmonth.

Private Edward DeWitt Patterson, Company D, Ninth Alabama Regiment, wrote in his diary that his Confederate comrades "have been traveling most of the day…with no other view than to show ourselves to the enemy, at as many different points of the line as possible." Confederate private J.W. Minnich described Magruder's numbers ruse as marching round, "bringing in regiments from less exposed positions on the line, marching them in a circle, as it were, all day emerging from the woods one part of the line, into the woods below… to appear again as fresh troops arriving."

In a similar account, Lieutenant Robert N. Miller of the Fourteenth Louisiana Regiment wrote his uncle Thomas F. Campbell: "The way Magruder fooled them was to divide each body of his troops [three regiments] in two parts and keep them travelling all the time for twenty four hours, till

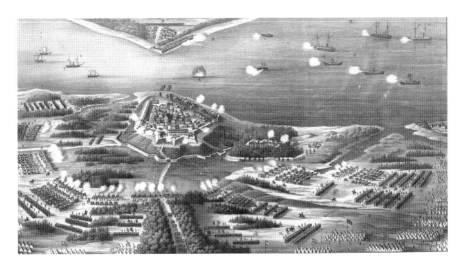

Sergeant Charles Worret, Twentieth New York Infantry Regiment, drew this bird's-eye view of the siege of Yorktown in April 1862 onsite. *Library of Congress.*

reinforcements came. The 14 La Regm't travelled from Yorktown to the right flank on the James [about nine miles] six times." Celebrated southern diarist Mary Chesnut's account also recalled Magruder's deception: "It was a wonderful thing how he played his ten thousand before like fireflies and utterly deluded him."

Other factors caused McClellan not to rush into battle. The Union maps of the peninsula between the James and York Rivers were not up to date. For example, the Warwick River was thought to run north–south on the peninsula, but it actually ran east–west. This posed significant problems for strategy and logistical planning.

McClellan faced three successive defensive lines across the peninsula. The first line began at Young's Mill. A more elaborate series of second defensive works faced him from Mulberry Island on the James River across the peninsula to Skiffe's Creek, then on to Lee's Mill and the Warwick River. Finally, the twelve-mile defensive strip—the Warwick Line—was anchored at Yorktown.

East of Williamsburg, Confederate colonel Benjamin Stoddert Ewell (president of the College of William and Mary before the war) erected a line of redoubts and rifle pits between the James and York Rivers. At the center was Fort Magruder, commanding a vital crossroads.

There was also Confederate subterfuge. Magruder ordered trees felled and logs from them painted black and mounted on redoubts and placed with

Famed photographer Mathew Brady took this image of John B. Magruder just prior to the Civil War when he was a brevet lieutenant colonel in the U.S. Army. He became a major general later in the Confederate army. *Courtesy of the Central Rappahannock Heritage Center.*

real artillery weapons. This misleading tactic was designed to exaggerate the strength of the emplacements.

The overly cautious McClellan decided not to attack; rather, he suspended his march toward Richmond and "settled in for a siege at Yorktown" on the battlefield where the culminating conflict of the American Revolution had been fought eighty-one years earlier. The siege lasted nearly a month as additional troops were added on both sides. Eventually, an estimated 120,000 Union troops faced not more than 56,000 Confederates.

This standoff stalled McClellan's plan to attack Richmond by moving his army from Fort Monroe, seventy-five miles east of the Confederate capital. McClellan's army began to move up the peninsula on April 4, 1862, going past Big Bethel and Young's Mill, previously occupied Confederate works. After going about twenty miles, the troops ran into the only Southern force standing in the way—Magruder's Army of the Peninsula—and the Warwick Line of redoubts and rifle pits.

On April 6, President Abraham Lincoln telegraphed McClellan and bluntly told him: "You now have over one hundred thousand troops…I think you better break the enemies' line from York-town to the Warwick River, at once." As of April 9, however, McClellan was not actively engaged with the Confederates. Lincoln wrote him again, pleading: "[I]t is indispensable to

After the siege, the Union army gathered material on the beach—cannonballs (*foreground*) and cannons (*middle*)—to send on ships up the York River to supply the Federals in the attack on Richmond. *Library of Congress.*

you that you strike a blow. I am powerless to help this…the present hesitation to move upon an intrenched [*sic*] enemy is but the story of Manassas repeated…but you must act." McClellan overestimated the Confederate troop strength and called for more forces, war materiel and supplies.

Meanwhile, skirmishes along the Warwick Line continued. Significant resistance from Confederate forces compelled Union brigadier general Erasmus D. Keyes to write McClellan from his headquarters below the Warwick Line: "Magruder is in a strongly fortified position behind the Warwick River, the fords to which have been destroyed by dams, and the approaches to which are through dense forests, swamps, and marshes. No part of this line as discovered can be taken without an enormous waste of life."

The severest early Union activity took place on April 16, when soldiers under Brigadier General William F. "Baldy" Smith ventured to harass Confederate troops at Dam No. 1 on the Warwick River. Smith's instructions were to avoid an engagement; rather, he was to "hamper" the enemy's efforts to strengthen its defensive works. Suddenly, Union troops achieved a breakthrough. But McClellan, who was on the scene, failed to order reinforcements. When the Confederates counterattacked, the Warwick River line was reestablished. Had Union reinforcements been able to breach the line, thousands of soldiers, moving westward, would have cut off Yorktown.

As the siege of Yorktown continued, Confederate president Jefferson Davis, in Richmond, urged his commander, General Johnston, whose troops were northwest of Richmond, to march to aid Magruder. Robert E. Lee, then Davis's chief military advisor, agreed. Eventually, more than 25,000 troops were sent to Yorktown. When Johnston arrived, he took overall command, with Magruder assuming command of a division of Johnston's army. McClellan vainly tried to ascertain exactly how many troops he faced. He even employed Professor Thaddeus S.C. Lowe to send balloons skyward to locate the Confederate positions. The Federals positioned more than seventy heavy guns in place.

As the siege wore on, it became more and more obvious that control of Yorktown was doomed. Confederate major general Daniel Harvey Hill, whose commanded fortified both sides of the York River, stressed that McClellan could "multiply his artillery indefinitely, and as his is so superior to ours, the result of such a fight cannot be doubtful." One of Hill's subordinates, Brigadier General Gabriel J. Rains, predicted that as many as three hundred shells per minute could fall once the big Union siege guns began firing.

These thirteen-inch mortars were part of Federal Battery No. 4 with officers of the First Connecticut Heavy Artillery. Photograph by James F. Gibson on Mathew Brady's staff. *Library of Congress.*

Johnston never wanted to defend Yorktown. He believed the position was indefensible. He felt strongly that fortifications were weak and faulty, with both flanks vulnerable and easily outmaneuvered by the Union navy on either the York or James River. Johnston told President Davis that Yorktown could not be held, but after a council of war Davis directed Johnston to defend the town.

During the last week of April, McClellan was positioning more than 110 heavy siege guns along with 300 smaller field guns. If unleashed, they could demolish the Confederate batteries and defenses. On April 29, 1862, Johnston notified Lee, "we must abandon the Peninsula soon." He noted that the fight for Yorktown "must be one of artillery, in which we cannot win. The result is certain; the time only doubtful."

Johnston ordered a withdrawal, but not before the Confederate artillery opened up a massive barrage against McClellan's batteries on Saturday,

Union soldiers on guard at the Sally Port in the center of the southwest point of entrenchments surrounding the town in May 1862. *Library of Congress.*

After the siege, a Union officer stands on the edge of a muddy dirt street inside Yorktown. The Yorktown Custom House is on the left, and the Cole Digges House is the first building on the right. *Library of Congress.*

May 3, and on into the evening. The shells were not concentrated on any particular target but unleashed at random.

François d'Orléans, Prince of Joinville, observed the scene: "The shells from the rifled guns flew in all directions with a length of range which had not before been suspected." George Thomas Stevens, a New York Seventy-Seventh Regiment surgeon, reported: "From one end of the line to the other the shells and shot poured into our campus, and the arches of fire that marked the courses of the shells, with flame spouting from the mouths of the guns created a magnificent pyrotechnic display." As darkness covered the battlefield, the bombardment suddenly ended.

Slowly through the night, the Confederates quietly and stealthy withdrew in two columns to the west toward Williamsburg. The rural roads were muddy, soaked after a week of rain, and wagons and artillery caissons bogged down. Some artillery pieces had to be abandoned on the road and even in place within old batteries.

A Union balloon sent up very early on May 4 revealed that the Confederates were gone. Union soldiers, seeing no action several hundred yards before them, crept from their rifle pits to find no enemy at all. They had vanished.

As the Confederates withdrew from Yorktown, they left behind little booby traps to surprise the oncoming Federal forces. Chief among these were torpedoes, better known today as land mines, developed by General Rains. This was the first successful use of the subterranean weapon by any troops during the Civil War, according to historian and mine warfare expert Norman Youngblood. Basically, they were crude explosive devices made from artillery shells or other materials that troops of Rains's hid around cannons and breastworks and left on roadways during the retreat.

"Wherever a torpedo had been buried, a short stick or branch was standing up, and woe to the man or animal who tread on it or kicked it," Union private Alfred Bellard wrote in his diary. In a report to Major General Hill, Rains wrote that "at a salient angle, an accessible point of our works, as part of the defenses thereof, I had the land mined with the weapons alluded to, to destroy assailants." Union officials were distraught when the mines began to injure and kill their soldiers. In fact, after the Battle of Williamsburg, when mines were found in the roadways, captured Confederate soldiers were forced to scour the paths to eliminate the torpedoes before the Federal troops proceeded.

Union troops caught up with the last elements of Johnston's retreating army just east of Williamsburg, and on May 5, a daylong battle was

A detail of the Winslow Homer painting *Rainy Day in Camp*, which shows Union soldiers outside Yorktown in April 1862. *Courtesy of the Metropolitan Museum of Art.*

fought, bloody but inconclusive, as Johnston withdraw and McClellan plodded behind.

The siege of Yorktown allowed the Confederates to buy time. McClellan's month-long hesitation gave Southern troops extra weeks to enhance defensive lines east of Richmond—lines that would be tested later in June.

12

BALLOONS OVER YORKTOWN

Wagons rumbled across a field not far from the remnants of Revolutionary War fortifications. These army war carts were unusual in their contents: balloons and the necessary equipment to fly them.

It was about noon on April 5, 1862, near the end of the first year of the Civil War. The Army of the Potomac was encamped at Yorktown in an effort to dislodge Confederate troops there and continue its drive up the Virginia Peninsula toward the Confederate capital of Richmond about fifty-five miles westward.

The balloons were a new element in the Union army arsenal that leaders hoped could help to more swiftly end the war. The balloons were never intended to drop munitions but rather were for observation. "Aeronauts" at the end of the tether could view a battlefield up to fifteen miles away and detect enemy actions and how troops were arrayed.

Demonstrations of the balloons took place around Washington, D.C., including one in June 1861 that sent a telegraph message from the balloon basket five hundred feet above the Columbia Armory (now the site of the National Air and Space Museum) to a room in the White House. The display got the attention of President Abraham Lincoln; by August, Thaddeus S.C. Lowe had received funds from the Union army to build a balloon corps.

Lowe, as the army's "Chief Aeronaut," arranged for the purchase of seven balloons, twelve field generators and a flattop barge to carry the equipment. With the equipment in hand, Lowe persuaded Gideon Wells,

Right: Professor Thaddeus S.C. Lowe commanded the Union army's balloon corps at Yorktown. *Library of Congress*.

Below: Union soldiers help tether Thaddeus Lowe's balloon in the spring of 1862. The basket in which Lowe is riding came up only to his knees and could hold only two people. *Library of Congress*.

secretary of the navy, to lend the army the barge—the renovated steamer *George Washington Park Custis*, the so-called first aircraft carrier. Lowe then was able to conduct exercises along the Potomac River from October 1861 to March 1862. Then it was time to put the enterprise into action. The barge went down the Potomac and the Chesapeake Bay to Fortress Monroe.

General George McClellan, who strongly supported the aerial observation concept, ordered a wagon train mobilized. Four wagons and two gas generators made their way up from Monroe to the Union forces encamped at Yorktown. Within a few hours of arrival, Lowe had one of the smaller balloons in the air. His bivouac area was adjacent to a sawmill located at Major General Samuel P. Heintzelman's headquarters only two miles from Yorktown.

"Each flight near Yorktown was an adventure. Civilian balloon flights were fraught with danger by themselves; military balloon flights magnified that danger," retired Army command sergeant major and historian James Clifford reflected. Portable hydrogen gas generators powered the Federal hot-air balloons.

Union brigadier general Fitz John Porter, in charge of the Yorktown siege, took his turn early on the morning of April 11, 1862, in the observation gondola of the balloon *Intrepid*. The wind came up, however, and the mooring line of Porter's balloon snapped; he began to drift over the Confederate lines. The men on the ground were helpless as sharpshooters attempted to bring the aircraft down.

Porter carefully reconnoitered the Confederate works below him as the balloon drifted along. When finally back over Union lines, he descended and immediately reported to General McClellan what he had seen. He was even able to report on Confederate guns at Gloucester Point across the river from Yorktown. Union balloonists ascended into the skies above Yorktown frequently during the monthlong encampment; among the officers who took to the air was Lieutenant George Armstrong Custer, who later excelled in Civil War battles and died on June 25, 1876, at the Battle of the Little Bighorn during the Indian Wars.

"The Federals had been using balloons in examining our positions, and we watched with envious eyes their beautiful observation as they floated high up in the air and well out of the range of our guns. We longed for the balloons that poverty denied us," wrote Confederate major general James Longstreet. At the time, he was on the staff of General Johnston in the breastworks defending the York River community and penned the observation in the *Century Magazine* more than twenty-five years later.

Left: Union brigadier general Fitz John Porter was commander of the Yorktown siege. *Library of Congress*.

Right: Union major general Samuel P. Heintzelman was on the fateful flight with Lowe that discovered the Confederate retreat on May 4, 1862. *Library of Congress*.

Across the battle lines, the Confederates probably had only one primitive balloon that was inflated using burning pine knots soaked in turpentine and its smoke. The trips, however, lasted only a short time because the hot air cooled quickly and became denser.

General Johnston was fortunate to find John Randolph Bryan, a captain from Gloucester County and an aide-de-camp of Major General John B. "Prince John" Magruder, head of the Army of the Peninsula. Bryan had volunteered to handle the balloon because he knew the area's terrain. He made a number of flights and, like General Porter, found himself free-flying one flight. The tether rope had been cut to free the leg of a solder whose limb had been tangled as Bryan ascended.

Bryan floated over the adjacent Union lines and, with a wind change, suddenly reversed course. Confederate troops, thinking it was a Union airship, opened fire. Fortunately for Bryan, the balloon was not hit. He eventually sailed over the York River and landed safely.

Frank Leslie's Illustrated newspaper artist Arthur Lumley went aloft in Professor Thaddeus Lowe's balloon in April 1862 and made this sketch of Confederate forts and camps. Lumley added the balloon to his drawing to show that the view was from about one thousand feet in the air. *National Air and Space Museum.*

Aeronaut Lowe and other observers routinely flew directly over the Southern positions at altitudes of between one and two thousand feet during good weather. On bad weather days, the balloon would remain over the Union lines only five hundred feet in the air. That way, Lowe and his crew seemed like a "traditional lookout but on an aerial platform."

The most militarily important Union balloon flight and "one of Lowe's most brilliant observation corps," according to aerial historian Richard Holmes, took place in the early-morning hours of May 4, 1862. Corporal Henry Alexander Scandrett of the Seventieth New York Infantry Regiment wrote in a newly found diary: "the Rebels were firing until half past four this morning. A balloon reconnaissance discovered the evacuation about 6 o'clock."

General Johnston had decided that his forces could not stand an all-out siege with its constant artillery barrages. He therefore ordered an immediate withdraw toward Williamsburg and then on to the defensive lines already erected outside Richmond.

McClellan thought the Confederate troops were being resupplied. With Lowe on the flight that morning was General Heintzelman. A quick view seemed to underscore the supply notation; however, Lowe looked more closely and saw "that the ingoing wagons were light and moved rapidly, while the outgoing wagons were heavily loaded and moved slowly, there was no longer any doubt as to the object of the Confederates. They were withdrawing," Lowe wrote later. General McClellan received that information from Lowe and Heintzelman, who reported, "We could not distinguish any guns or men in or around the fortifications of Yorktown. The smoke of [the Rebel] camp was very much diminished."

Lowe's last recorded Yorktown observation was, "We…saw our troops advance upon the empty works, throwing out their skirmishers, and feeling their way as if expecting to meet the enemy." Within hours, the Confederates were nearly at Williamsburg, but the Federal troops were close behind and made contact with Longstreet's rear guard in the early hours of May 5. The result was the Battle of Williamsburg.

There are conflicting reports that a Confederate balloon, known by some as the "Silk Dress Balloon," could have been flown by Bryan over Yorktown in the early days of May, but most probably it was not used until the Seven Days campaign outside of Richmond later in June. Nevertheless, a romantic legend—that the colorful balloon was made from Southern ladies' dresses donated for the patriotic cause—has grown up around the balloon.

General Longstreet in 1886 encouraged the legend when he wrote that the word was sent out "to gather together all the silk dresses in the Confederacy and make a balloon. It was done, as soon we had a great patchwork ship of many and varies hues…and was ready for use." However, this was not true. Dresses were not used, but rather the material came from various bolts of new silk secured around Savannah, Georgia, and manufactured by Dr. Edward Cheves. It was then sent to General Robert E. Lee "for use in reconnoitering the enemy's lines.

The multicolored Confederate balloon, named *Gazelle*, was last operated on the outskirts of Richmond. Lieutenant Colonel Edward Porter Alexander used it during the Battle of Seven Pines. Subsequently, the Confederates moved their airship operations to the James River, where it was loaded on the *Teaser*, an armed tug.

With the *Gazelle* on board, the *Teaser* ran aground on a sandbar and was captured by USS *Maratanza*, a vessel of the Union navy. Colored pieces of the balloon later were divided up and given as souvenirs to Union government officials.

After Yorktown, the Union balloon corps traveled up the York and Pamunkey Rivers on the flatboat and then was moved inland. Lowe operated balloons—the large *Intrepid* and smaller *Constitution*—during several battles around Richmond in June and July 1862.

Unfortunately, Lowe became ill with malaria in the summer and returned to Washington. After his recovery, he found that all the service equipment, wagons and mules had been returned to the army quartermaster. His balloon corps had dissipated and was never again used in an active campaign by the Union military.

13

SLABTOWN

An African American Community

For more than a century, from 1863 to 1975, Slabtown, an African American settlement, occupied a portion of the famed Yorktown battlefield, where, in 1781, American independence was won.

The community, established in 1863, began as a home for freed slaves. Slabtown—Uniontown, as it was later called—was a vibrant neighborhood. At one time, there were almost as many houses in Slabtown as there were in the nearby predominately white village of Yorktown.

Nearly in the heart of the Yorktown battlefield, not far from reconstructed eighteenth-century earthworks, a narrow, deteriorating roadway winds through the woods and a bushy field. It is all that is left of Slabtown, which thrived here until the mid-1970s.

Early in May 1862, following the Confederate withdrawal, black citizens flocked to the area, both from York County and from adjacent Virginia locales, seeking protection by Federal troops. They camped any way possible as their numbers rapidly increased. Brigadier General Isaac Jones Wistar, in his autobiography, describes Yorktown after his late 1862 visit. The military camp—Fort Yorktown—was run-down and "the most disgusting I have ever seen in a military post," he writes. The general estimates "12,000 refugee Negroes supported in idleness on Government rations, and lying about without order under any ragged shelter they could get in, in every stage of filth, poverty, disease and death."

Wistar's first mission was to clean up the area. The existing fortifications were cleared so a minimum military force could maintain them. He found "a

Slabtown, or Uniontown, is located amid trees in the center just below the golf course in this 1920s aerial view of the Yorktown battlefield. *National Park Service, Colonial National Historical Park.*

large area of abandoned fields a few miles in the rear" suitable for refugees' encampment. The land, Wistar reports, "was surveyed and laid out in two- and four-acre lots, with street and building lines; and all the able bodied negroes set to work building log cabins of prescribed form and dimensions." Soldiers dubbed the new village Slabtown because its buildings primarily were constructed "from the numerous slabs of wood lying about the field." The slabs were the outside remains after trees were sawed into timbers. Some were simply log cabins.

Later, some of the traditional shotgun houses—one-room wide with a gabled front with other rooms arranged to the rear—were built. Initially, one hundred homes were constructed to house six hundred people. Each family had a good-sized lot where they could cultivate gardens or raise livestock. Later, there may have been as many as four hundred cabins.

Wistar expresses amazement at the success of Slabtown. The community "had become large and populous, and was clean, quiet, and to a considerable extent self-supporting. It was well-policed by a small force of selected Negroes, chosen by the Provost Marshal, and the most capable residents were from time to time placed on abandoned and unoccupied farming-lands outside the town," he writes.

In an extensive research paper on Slabtown, historian Dr. Kelley Deetz explains that it "had six freedmen's schools, more than any other Black community....A daily average of 400 students attended the day schools. Night schools educated Slabtown's adult population as well." A church, ultimately named Shiloh Baptist Church, was established on the edge of the town. It was described as a "log church covered with straight up and down boards," according to the church history.

Slabtown's residents supported themselves on their own land and by their various trades—woodcutters, shoemakers, carpenters, farmers, watermen, laborers and even storekeepers and two milkmen, according to an 1872 survey of African American males in the area. Through the years, most Slabtown residents gained title to their land. "The community interacted with surrounding black settlements," such as the ones in York County at Acreville (now part of the Yorktown Naval Weapons Station) on the York River above Yorktown, at Lackey west of Yorktown and at Grove in James City County.

In 1895, John W. Shaw, superintendent of Yorktown National Cemetery, wanted a monument erected commemorating the Yorktown surrender site. He selected a location near the existing national cemetery and adjacent to an African American cemetery and Slabtown. He built a monument—a twenty-two-foot brick obelisk covered by painted stucco.

Within a decade of its dedication, the monument fell into disrepair. The local chapter of the Daughters of the American Revolution (DAR) was convinced it was not located in the actual surrender spot. In 1934, the obelisk was taken down and left in nearby woods, where it lay until 2013, when it was finally destroyed. Sarah Goldberger, a historian who has studied Yorktown's monuments extensively, suggests one reason it was removed dealt with its proximity to Slabtown and the adjacent Union and African American cemeteries.

Significant changes came to York County African Americans as a result of World War I. With the nearby deepwater port at the mouth of the Chesapeake Bay, the federal government began condemning large chunks of acreage along the York River for navy use. These were neighborhoods with hundreds of African Americans, including the aforementioned Acreville, but Slabtown to the east was spared.

In 1930, Congress authorized the National Park Service to secure property and create the Colonial National Monument on land around the Victory

This obelisk originally was erected to mark the site of the surrender field. It was determined later that the location was wrong and was moved, in part, probably because it was adjacent to Slabtown. *From the collection of Richard Shisler, Yorktown, Virginia.*

Monument, the decorative column erected in the 1880s just outside the village of Yorktown. At about the same time, plans were underway for the sesquicentennial celebration at Yorktown in October 1931. Uniontown, as it was known then—home to mainly working-class folks who lived in improved houses—was located in the woods and fields adjacent to the celebration site. It was not part of the property purchases. This is possibly because the community was considered to be of little consequence, but more likely because federal funds were limited due to the Great Depression. Within a few years, the Colonial National Monument became Colonial National Historical Park, with 4,500 acres of land designated to form the park. But funding was limited, and Uniontown was not threatened.

World War II forced the federal government to increase activities at various nearby naval installations; again, more property was secured, but Uniontown remained secure. However, by the mid-1960s, children of the older Uniontown citizens found it impossible to get a building permit to construct their own homes, either on their parents' land or on adjacent property. Floyd E. Hill Jr. found himself in such a plight in 1965. "I wanted to build my own home, but they wouldn't give me a building permit. I couldn't get a permit from anybody," he explained.

York County was reluctant to issue the permits, "because I figured they knew the government wanted the property. There were lots of talk flying around then about Uniontown being taken over," Hill added. At no time,

These homes were part of Slabtown, or Uniontown, just before they were demolished. *National Park Service, Colonial National Historical Park.*

he stressed, was the community decaying. "Nothing was a disgrace to look at. There were some shacks there, but they were painted and kept up." In addition to housing, the community also had "three shot houses" or "juke joints" in the mid-twentieth century. These small buildings provided music, a place to socialize and alcohol, Hill explained.

In the 1960s, Uniontown was surrounded by federal property—the park service and a U.S. Coast Guard station. Hill recalled that in his youth there was a nearby golf course—all that remained of the Yorktown Manor Hotel project begun in the 1920s. "There were several of the holes right behind my folks' home. Sometimes my daddy and I would caddy, and other times late in the day I would go out and hit a ball over maybe the 7th, 8th and 9th fairways [that once were part of the battlefield]. I wouldn't go near the clubhouse because I wasn't supposed to play on the course." It was a "whites only" facility. (The hotel was never completed, and the project went bankrupt. The steel skeleton of the big building was still visible until about 1940, and the eighteen-hole golf course near the river lasted a little longer.)

The U.S. government's purchase of land in Uniontown began slowly, but life dramatically changed in 1974 when Congress authorized funds for the National Park Service to purchase the community's 115 acres. With money in hand, the U.S. Department of the Interior sent letters to Uniontown residents, Dr. Deetz explained, "stating that they were in the process of obtaining their privately owned property as part of the land acquisition program" for the historical park. Under governmental

Floyd E. Hill Jr. was born in Slabtown and lived there for many years. *Courtesy of Floyd E. Hill Jr.*

regulations, residents were obligated to accept the offers of "fair market value established by independent appraisal."

This was at a time when plans were well underway for the national independence bicentennial celebration to be held at numerous national parks and historic sites. Yorktown was to be the center of the festivities in 1981. No one—except the Uniontown residents—wanted the community on the edge of the battlefield during the festivities. Ostensibly, the park service said it wanted to restore the original Revolutionary War earthworks that were in the area and construct a new road. Neither earthworks nor road, however, was ever built.

In describing Uniontown as he remembered, Hill explained: "Most of those homes did not have running water or a sewer system Almost all had their own wells, some had septic tanks, but most had just privies [outhouses] near the woods. But most important—the residents owned the land and they owned their homes. Some folks owed money on them, but not much. Most of the land has been passed down through families."

Troy Griffin no longer lives in Virginia, but he still returns to York County to visit relatives, many of whom still talk about Slabtown. "I am an original family member of Slabtown," he explained. "My mother and father and grandparents are buried there to this day. I remember playing with my Matchbox cars when I was five or six. I used to play all over the battlefield until we left."

Ethel Braxton Curtis, Troy Griffin's aunt, grew up in the historic black community. In an article in the Newport News *Daily Press*, she explains: "This was a neighborhood where we all looked out for each other—and where just about everyone was related. So when we had to move, it was not a very easy time for people who had put down such strong roots."

Griffin said the government talked about Slabtown as an "eyesore" and they came through with "divide and conquer" tactics to take the land. "Once one person sold others thought they had to sell. Many didn't want to do it, but they had to sell or the property was condemned." Homes were purchased, and the government agreed to help relocate persons within the same general area; there also was relocation money available. For many, explained Hill,

Ethel Braxton Curtis, longtime Slabtown resident, stands in a field where the African American community stood before the National Park Service razed it. *Courtesy of the Newport News* Daily Press, *photo by Aileen Devlin.*

whose father was one of the last to leave in 1977, "the relocations hurt. Our community was gone."

Looking today at the old Slabtown site, it is not difficult for historians to remember that General Wistar's Slabtown provided generations of African Americans with a homestead and a strong sense of community.

14

SHILOH BAPTIST CHURCH FOUNDED IN 1863

Wahen visitors came to the Yorktown battlefield in 1881 to commemorate the one hundredth anniversary of the British surrender to the American and French forces, no one noticed or cared about a nearby rustic cabin of an African American Baptist church building or the fact that its congregation had begun amid the tumultuous Civil War.

The celebration was about the Revolutionary War, but for almost a century, Shiloh Baptist Church, situated on the battlefield, played an important role in Yorktown's history as well as in the social and political fabric of York County.

In 1863, after the Confederate army withdrew from Yorktown, former slaves sought refuge at Fort Yorktown, the defensive fortifications left by Southern troops. The newly freed African Americans wanted to shape their own religious emphasis and founded a church within their community of Slabtown. The church became a center of social activity and political discussions, including meetings regarding the state of freedmen. It survived as a dominant player during Reconstruction and, later, the dark days of segregation and discrimination. In the 1960s and '70s, the congregation led the desegregation fight.

Slabtown resident, former slave and lay minister John Carey joined with the Reverend Jeremiah W. Asher to encourage the establishment of a church. Reverend Asher, one of the first African American chaplains in the Union army, was in Yorktown by December 1863 with the Sixth U.S. Colored

The Reverend Jeremiah W. Asher was cofounder of Shiloh Baptist Church in Slabtown in 1863. *Courtesy of Shiloh Baptist Church, Philadelphia, Pennsylvania.*

Infantry Regiment. Before the war, he was a prominent abolitionist; since 1849, he had served as minister of Shiloh Baptist Church in Philadelphia, Pennsylvania.

A Connecticut-born free African American, Asher took an interest in the young Carey and became a devoted friend and ally. They frequently talked about religion and how a church could help the community. In December 1863, Carey and Asher founded the new church. Unfortunately, Asher's unit moved only four months later, in April 1864. That first church building was described as "a log church covered with straight up and down boards."

The name *Shiloh* honors the Reverend Asher's Philadelphia church. (In biblical terms, *Shiloh* means "The one to whom it belongs" and is a prophetic name for the Messiah.) The Reverend Carey became the church's first pastor. It was located near the missionary house of the Quakers. They came to Yorktown in November 1863 intent on bringing a variety of programs to aid the freedmen. This "Friends' Association" established in Philadelphia sent seventeen volunteer teachers to Slabtown. The Quakers frequently attended services at Shiloh, according to a research study by historian Dr. Kelley Deetz.

Sarah Cadberry, a teacher who arrived in March 1866, kept a diary of her experiences and wrote favorably about the church's programs and ministers. Preaching, she said, was presented in "a simple hearty way." One night, Cadberry observed a room full of people and a lone couple dancing. "These dance-hymns are very musical and the jumping motion often very graceful." In general, Dr. Deetz concluded that Cadbury "believed she was witnessing a religious revival at Slabtown [and] made numerous references to devout children who spent all of their time praying."

Brothers Daniel M. Norton and Robert Norton were members and trustees of the young church. Both were former slaves who had escaped from Virginia to New York in the 1850s, returning to the Yorktown area at the end of the Civil War. Daniel set up his medical practice in Yorktown, and Robert was a storekeeper and sometime farmer. The brothers used Shiloh Church as their base for a secret "beneficial" organization—the Lone Star Society—to support their political activities. On July 4, 1871, an estimated seven thousand persons staged a parade in Yorktown sponsored by the society.

Daniel and Robert Norton were elected to many terms in the Virginia General Assembly. Daniel served in the Virginia Senate from York County from 1871 to 1873 and from 1877 to 1887. Robert served in the Virginia House of Delegates from York County from 1869 to 1882, except for one two-year term. A younger brother, Frederick S. Norton, also was elected to the house from the Williamsburg–James City County district for a two-year term beginning in 1869.

In 1893, Shiloh moved across the maturing Slabtown community to a new site near the Yorktown National Cemetery. The new church, however, burned in 1897. Trustee Daniel Norton was among those who immediately came forward financially to help rebuild. According to church records, the stately sanctuary cost $9,000 to build. (In 2018 terms, $258,500.)

Robert Norton and his brother Daniel served as trustees of Shiloh Baptist Church. Robert used the church as the activity center for the Lone Star Society. *Special Collections and Archives, Virginia State University.*

That third structure, with its cornerstone laid in 1898, was a distinctive white frame building with a stately bell tower. The entryway was situated at the base of the tower adjacent to the sanctuary. Daniel Norton bought the beautiful stained-glass windows that were installed. "The architectural design of the Old Shiloh was quite different from that of most churches of that period, and every day was admired by visitors to Yorktown," the Reverend Richard Holmes wrote in a Shiloh history.

Times and life changed by 1931, when the nation celebrated the 150th anniversary of the Battle of Yorktown. An amphitheater and stage and an array of tents were erected on the battlefield for the festivities. Not far away was the church building, but neither the congregation nor the building was considered part of the fete. Because the church was not of the Revolutionary War era, it was simply ignored.

The National Park Service's Colonial National Historical Park began to grow around Slabtown and Shiloh Church with the purchase of property to protect the battlefield site. About 1970, Congress appropriated funds to begin acquisition of Slabtown. The church building and its land were purchased in 1971 by Colonial National Historical Park when it was determined that portions of the battlefield in that area would be rebuilt. The congregation was paid $17,000 for the property and given 3.4 acres at the intersection of Goosley Road and U.S. Route 17.

Ronald Muse, a young member who studied construction planning, drew a number of sketches of a proposed church, and the trustees finally made

This postcard shows Shiloh Baptist Church at Slabtown prior to 1970, when the National Park Service purchased the property. *Courtesy of Shiloh Baptist Church.*

a selection. An architect was hired to put Muse's plan into blueprint form. Charles Richardson of Hampton, Virginia, was the general contractor. Construction of the new church building cost $175,000 (about $1 million in 2018).

The ground-breaking ceremony was held on December 18, 1971, and the new structure was dedicated on December 23, 1973. The valuable stained-glass windows from the old church were prominently placed in the new sanctuary. As part of the transition from old to new, the congregation met at Old Shiloh for a morning service conducted by its pastor, the Reverend Richard Holmes, and then marched to the new church for its dedication. The Reverend W.J. Beckett, former Shiloh pastor, preached the dedication sermon.

Charles E. Brown, past president of the Virginia chapter of the National Association for the Advancement of Colored People (NAACP) and a member of Shiloh for more than fifty years, was chairman of the board of trustees in 1974. In those days, he said, when he thought of the church, "my mind does not dwell too long upon the church building, but rather upon the old heralds of the Cross"—those men and women who began the church in the early days following the Emancipation Proclamation of January 1, 1863.

Shiloh Baptist Church, with its historic stained-glass windows, was erected in 1973. *Photo by the author.*

The park service's $17,000 was hardly a down payment for the cost of the new church building. The financial gamble to secure a loan paid off; through the years, fish fries, bake sales, spaghetti dinners and some faithful donors helped raise money to pay off the debt.

On July 21, 2013, Shiloh Baptist, along with the Colonial National Historical Park, celebrated the 150th anniversary of Slabtown and the founding of the church. A worship service was held at Shiloh, followed by lunch, as part of the church's anniversary homecoming program. Later in the afternoon, many congregation members, some of whom had lived in Slabtown, walked the half-mile route from the current church to the site of Old Shiloh and its adjacent church cemetery, where a wreath was laid. In addition, a roll call was conducted of U.S. Colored Troops from the Civil War buried in Yorktown National Cemetery. Wreaths and flowers were placed in the cemetery.

During the anniversary program, the National Park Service, for the first time, unveiled an informational sign about Shiloh Baptist Church and Slabtown; the sign was placed adjacent to the national cemetery and across from the old church site. Church members are proud that the growth of their congregation in the last decade has been outstanding, perhaps the best in its long history. A homecoming program is held annually in October, and members still walk back to the old church site on the battlefield to rekindle their historical heritage.

15

GRAND 1881 CENTENNIAL CELEBRATION

The centennial of the British surrender at Yorktown almost did not have its superstar. President James A. Garfield had died just twenty-nine days before the national celebration was to begin.

Inaugurated on March 4, 1881, Garfield agreed to participate in the Yorktown festivities during a summer meeting with John Goode Jr. of Virginia, the outgoing chairman of the House of Representatives' centennial committee. Goode said Garfield's parting words to him were, "I shall meet you at Yorktown and you may expect me to make the effort of my life."

Garfield was shot on July 2 by an unhinged office seeker. He did not succumb to his wounds until September 19. For two months and eighteen days, the presidency hung in limbo—and so did planning for the Yorktown centennial.

Three days of celebratory events were to begin on October 18, a day ahead of the actually anniversary of the surrender by British general Charles, Lord Cornwallis, to American and French forces. There was concern that national mourning of Garfield's assassination would spread gloom over the event and that the new president might not attend.

Once Garfield's successor, Chester A. Arthur, took the oath of office, he recognized that a chief aim of celebrating the military end of the American Revolution was to heal the lingering breach between North and South caused by the Civil War. It was time for the nation to move forward.

Arthur also felt it was vital to handle Great Britain cautiously. New York senator Chancy Depew remembered: "The President, with characteristic grace and tact determined that the ceremonies should also officially record that all feelings of hostility against the mother country were dead." Nevertheless, no British representatives were invited. The president, however, did urge a special military salute honoring the British flag on the centennial's last day. According to professor and historian Dr. Julie Ann Sweet, "The salute was graceful and appropriate, and it demonstrated that the country could celebrate victory without overly glorifying the defeat of their enemy."

President Chester A. Arthur attended the 1881 Yorktown Centennial Celebration. *Library of Congress.*

In his first public ceremonial appearance, President Arthur gave the keynote speech on October 19. Although brief, his remarks focused on "the anniversary of independence and Union in spite of the Civil War, respect for England as a worthy and honorable enemy of the past, and appreciation for the help of the French allies without whom victory would not have been possible," Dr. Sweet explained. Specifically, Arthur intoned: "The resentments which attended, and for a time survived the clash of arms have long since ceased to animate our hearts. It is with no feeling of exultation over a defeated foe that to-day we summon up a remembrance of those events which have made holy the ground whereon we tread."

Arthur watched the elaborate military review from the grandstand and witnessed naval maneuvers from the embankment of the York River. He and members of his cabinet attended an elaborate Masonic ceremony laying the cornerstone of what would become the Yorktown Victory Monument. Arthur, however, did not participate, since he was not a Mason. "Fully clothed in ceremonial garb and extremely serious about their Masonic rituals, the Masons occupied much of the grandstand," Sweet wrote. The president departed via steamer late on October 20 for Washington.

Organizing the national celebration was a cumbersome, time-consuming task. On September 4, 1879, a York County committee initiated plans for the centennial, wanting to stage an elaborate program with the president and his cabinet in attendance. Later, a council of representatives from the original thirteen states convened in Philadelphia to push for a national event. Finally, the U.S. Congress sanctioned the event and partially paid the costs.

Yorktown, however, was not ready to serve as the host. The 1880 census reports only 251 people living in Yorktown proper in sixty-four households with just a few more males than females. There was no railroad, no regular steamboat service. "Yorktown is about as far from nowhere, and about as inaccessible, as any town east of the Sandwich Islands," historian Julius Rathbun reported. When it rained, the mud was two feet deep, and when it was dry, the dust was three feet deep, he added.

Virginia author Thomas Nelson Page, in *Scribner's Monthly* in October 1881, says, "Once more the sleepy [Yorktown], which has for a century lain as if under a spell, awakes with a start to find itself the center of interest." Looking at the town's landscape, Page wrote, "Even at this day the place gives evidence of its advantages as a fortified camp," left over from the Civil War years. "High ramparts and deep fosses…surround it on three sides and on the fourth, a precipitous bluff above the deep, wide York." The town's few buildings still give "the impressiveness of an old walled town. All new ways and things seem to have been held at bay."

Locally, the Yorktown Centennial Association was created as a joint stock company to try to secure funding for accommodations and military requirements. Also, Congress created its own Yorktown Congressional Centennial Committee. There was only one joint meeting of the two organizations; the separate groups went about their own planning efforts.

French officials were involved, including descendants of the Marquis de Lafayette and Comte de Rochambeau. German officials also attended, with descendants of Baron Friedrich Wilhelm von Steuben, the Prussian military officer who came to America to join George Washington's army and taught military drills and tactics.

Eventually, funds were appropriated to build a grandstand and a tent city. Many temporary frame structures, decorated with French and American

One of the few surviving photographs from the 1881 centennial shows the Masonic ceremony of the cornerstone-laying of the Yorktown Victory Monument. *National Park Service, Colonial National Historical Park.*

colors, were erected for vendors and bars. The Chesapeake & Ohio Railroad constructed a railroad spur from Lee Hall to Yorktown, enabling a few trains from Richmond and northward to access the area.

Most people came to Yorktown by river steamer and were day-trippers not wanting to stay in homes of residents or in the tent city overnight. Some people, especially those from Washington, D.C., spent the night aboard ships; the majority of Virginians came via train from Richmond to West Point and took a steamer down the York River to Yorktown.

According to contemporary accounts, the river adjacent to Yorktown was jammed with public and private vessels of all types and descriptions. Suggesting that "these waters may never again see so many craft collected together," a *New York Times* reporter questioned, "If Yorktown is destined to witness a second centennial, what sort of vessels will they be which will anchor off the bluffs in the year 19[8]1?"

Still, with just days to go before the celebration, the *New York Times* on October 12 lamented: "No adequate provision has yet been made for the 40,000 to 50,000 people who are expected to arrive next, if not this, week. Rooms are almost impossible to get.…All visitors to Yorktown this week or next should come prepared with blankets or rugs in case of need."

While the main celebration took place Tuesday through Thursday, October 18–20, programs began on Thursday, October 13. According to Dr. Sweet's research, the Moore House, in which the documents of surrender were negotiated, "was only open to last minute workmen" and not the public. Goode, the association president, "arrived to give the opening address, but no one came to listen to it."

Harper's Weekly, A Journal of Civilization carried an extensive, somewhat critical summary of the centennial. The unidentified author reported that the opening day "passed unmarked save by the hurly-burly of preparation… [and on the second day, October 14] addresses were to have been delivered by a number of distinguished gentlemen, none of whom appeared." A ball was to be held that night at the pavilion, which was not finished. Saturday was to feature a regatta with sailing and rowing, "with pyrotechnic displays and illuminations in the evening," *Harper's Weekly* noted. Neither event took place, "nor did the gentlemen of the committee make any apologies for the failure to provide the advertised amusements."

On Sunday, some scheduled events actually took place. There was a Catholic Mass, but a scheduled Protestant service was not held. The Moore House, however, finally opened with new paint, wallpaper and carpets. *Harper's Weekly* suggested that the refurbishment left the house "robbed

General view of the exhibition grounds and York River harbor. *From* Harper's Weekly, *October 29, 1881. From the author's collection.*

of the beauty and dignity of age by the hands of vandals who had dared desecrate it and *modernize* it."

Sunday also welcomed some rain, because the earlier weather produced much heat and "dust reigns supreme in the camp," the *New York Times* reported. But the remainder of the week returned to heat and dust. Monday's schedule was much fuller and began to form a celebration with a host of speeches.

President Arthur and his entourage arrived on Tuesday morning, when the program organized by the federal government began. The Masonic program was staged with speeches, prayers, music and the official cornerstone-laying for the Yorktown monument.

Wednesday was the one hundredth anniversary date and featured Arthur's remarks, musical presentations and addresses by foreign delegates, including M. Maxime Outrey speaking for the French government and Marquis de Rochambeau and Colonel von Steuben speaking on behalf of their families. Robert Charles Winthrop, former Speaker of the U.S. House of

Representatives and senator from Massachusetts, gave the oration of nearly two hours. James Barron Hope, considered by many to be Virginia's poet laureate, recited his own centennial poem. An elaborate fireworks display and a promenade concert concluded the day.

Major music for Tuesday's and Wednesday's programs was provided by the United States Marine Band led by John Philip Sousa, who later would be known as the "March King" for the approximately 130 military and patriotic marches he composed. He had joined the Marine Band in 1880 and would remain its director and composer until 1892. Sousa wrote the "Yorktown Centennial" march, probably for the celebration, but there is no record it was performed. Among his other famous marches are "Stars and Stripes Forever," "Semper Fidelis," "The Liberty Bell" and "The Washington Post."

Thursday, October 20, the celebration's final day, involved both naval and military reviews. In front of the grandstand, more than nine thousand men marched, representing all aspects of the military—regular army units, state guard units and local units, such as the Wise Light Infantry of Williamsburg, Richmond Light Infantry Blues and the Norfolk Light Artillery Blues.

When the celebration was over, Yorktown returned to its sleepy self. All the temporary facilities were removed within days. There were few favorable reviews, even from the Virginia newspapers.

Dr. Sweet, in her research report conclusion, notes that *Harper's Weekly* called the celebration a "failure." And one observer explained "in homely but forcible language" that the Yorktown Centennial Association (the local organization) had "bitten off a bigger hunk than [it] could chaw." The *Richmond Daily Dispatch*, two days after the close, apologized in its October 22 edition, saying that "our deeds have not filled the measure of our desires"

Yorktown military and naval reviews took place on October 20, the centennial's last day. *From* Harper's Weekly, *October 29, 1881. From the author's collection.*

A centennial celebration political cartoon, "All Hands Round." *From* Harper's Weekly, *October 29, 1881. From the author's collection.*

and lamenting that "our foreign guests will no doubt have much to recall of discomfort and inconvenience."

Even though criticism was abundant, the event not only pulled the North and South together but also reiterated America's ties with European allies, especially France. Perhaps a political cartoon in *Harper's Weekly* (October 22 edition) entitled "All Hands Round—at Yorktown, Virginia, October 19, 1881" says it best with images depicting Germany and France and the North and South dancing around the "corner stone of peace."

16

COLONIAL NATIONAL
HISTORICAL PARK

On July 6, 1881, the United States Congress authorized the purchase of a parcel of land "on a commanding hill overlooking the York River" for a monument. With that action, the federal government began its involvement with Yorktown, many years before the National Park Service was created.

A conflict arose in the planning stage when local citizens wanted the monument to be located near Yorktown and not on the battlefield, as envisioned by the federal government. The locals won out, and the current site of the grand Victory Monument was chosen. Its cornerstone was laid during an elaborate Masonic ceremony on October 18, 1881, as part of the Yorktown Centennial festivities. Chester A. Arthur, who had assumed the presidency of the United States only a month earlier, attended the program.

The idea of a monument had been in the making just ten days after the surrender of General Charles, Lord Cornwallis, and his British army in October 1781. The Continental Congress, meeting in Philadelphia, enacted a resolution directing that a marble column be erected "at York in Virginia" recognizing the American and French allied victory over the English.

Attempts in 1834, 1836 and 1876 were made to persuade Congress to act on the monument, but it was not until 1879 that Congress appointed a group to study the matter. Finally, in 1880, citizens of North Carolina added their voices to requests from Rhode Island and Virginia that Congress authorize funds for the project. Ultimately, the ninety-eight-foot-tall monument with

The Victory Monument was completed in 1884 and remains the centerpiece of the National Park Service's Yorktown component. *Photo by Ken Lund, Reno, Nevada.*

the figure of *Liberty* as its crowning glory was finished on August 12, 1884. The monument occupies Lot nos. 80–83 of the original 1691 Yorktown plat and remains "a fitting symbol" of the French and American alliance and victory, the park service emphasizes.

Lightning has struck the monument twice and done significant damage. On July 29, 1942, a bolt hit the figure of *Liberty* atop the marble column and sheared off its head and arms. A new figure by sculptor Oskar J.W. Hansen was finally in place in 1957. Another lightning bolt struck on June 30, 1990, but repairs were accomplished quickly. Efforts began in August 2018 to repair the monument and to either restore or replace the statue.

It was not, however, until 1930—nearly fifty years after the monument was erected—that the federal government embarked on a larger scheme to protect the adjacent battlefield and remaining structures of the colonial town of York. John D. Rockefeller Jr., who had agreed to fund the restoration of colonial-era Williamsburg, was a prime mover, along with William Carson, director of the Virginia Commission on Conservation and Development, and the Comte de Grasse chapter of the Daughter of the American Revolution. The project was an effort to increase Virginia tourism.

They convinced Horace Albright, second director of the National Park Service, to visit Yorktown, Williamsburg and Jamestown and offered that the creation of a Colonial National Monument at Yorktown "would be a great asset to both the area and the nation," author Frances Watson Clark wrote. "The groundwork [also] was set for a scenic road that would connect" the three major historic localities.

President Herbert Hoover proclaimed the establishment of the Colonial National Monument on December 30, 1930, "for the preservation of the historical structures and remains thereon and for the benefit and enjoyment of the people." The national monument became the Colonial National Historical Park in 1936.

The national park was to include Jamestown Island and eventually a "Colonial Parkway" linking Yorktown, Williamsburg and Jamestown, whose elements form today's Virginia Historic Triangle. Initially, the size of the monument was 1,296 acres of the Yorktown battlefield and 402 acres of the town; a five-hundred-foot right-of-way or 230 acres for the parkway; and almost all of Jamestown Island—1,561 acres, excluding 22 acres purchased in 1898 by the Association for the Preservation of Virginia Antiquities (now Preservation Virginia).

In June 1931, just a year after the national monument was created, two professionally trained historians—B. Floyd Flickinger, history instructor at the College of William and Mary, and Elbert Cox, a University of Virginia graduate student—began developing the historical program, according to the "Administrative History: Expansion of the National Park Service in the 1930s."

The historical program's objective was to "serve as a link to bind the past to the present and be a guide and an inspiration for the future." (Flickinger became acting superintendent of Colonial National Monument in August 1933 and superintendent of Colonial National Historical Park [December 1933 to May 1939].)

On June 5, 1936, the monument was re-designated a national park. Today, the park totals 9,271 federally owned acres at Yorktown, on Jamestown Island and on the connecting Colonial Parkway.

Part of the early park project was the construction of the parkway, a three-lane, twenty-three-mile scenic byway that is also an All-American Road, one of only thirty-one in the nation. It is toll-free, but semitrucks are not allowed. The center lane is used for selective passing. The initial segment of the parkway, which was designed to look like a country road, was begun in 1931 between Yorktown and Williamsburg and completed in

The Colonial National Monument was created in 1930. Sesquicentennial soldiers in colonial uniforms pose for an early photograph at a reconstructed redoubt. *Special Collections Research Center, Swem Library, College of William and Mary.*

1937. An important aspect of that link was the construction of a tunnel under Williamsburg's Historic Area, which was completed in 1942. World War II and "some structural and flooding problems" prevented the tunnel from opening until 1949. In the meantime, every year at the College of William and Mary's homecoming, sororities and fraternities used the tunnel as a place to build their parade floats during inclement weather.

The final parkway section between Williamsburg and Jamestown was completed in 1957, in time for the 350th anniversary of the Jamestown settlement. Although it took more than twenty-five years to complete the project, the second segment encompassed the same design standards as the initial road.

Local horticulture expert and self-taught brick-maker Paul Matthew Griesenauer made all the bricks for the construction of the bridges crossing the parkway from Yorktown to Williamsburg. He operated James Towne Collony, which produced pottery and bricks and in 1933 received the

The first section of the Colonial Parkway connected Yorktown and Williamsburg. This photograph, taken on August 10, 1934, shows the Rex machine laying concrete for the three-lane roadway. *National Park Service, Colonial National Historical Park.*

contract to produce the much-needed "colonial-era" bricks. Griesenauer's clay came from the banks of the James River, not many miles from historic Jamestown. He took time and effort to try to duplicate the glazed headers needed for bricks, to resemble those used in the area during colonial times. The results still survive in the bridges over the parkway.

In addition to the roadway, the federal government also began to purchase much of the area that comprised the town of York, including some of the surviving colonial-era structures. Today, the National Park Service owns the Nelson House, the Dudley Digges House, the Cole Digges House (formerly known as the Thomas Pate House), the Ballard House, the Edmund Smith House and the Somerwell House. The park service has reconstructed Dr. Corbin Griffith's Medical Shop and the Swan Tavern on their original sites. Several other colonial homes survived and are in private hands, including the Sessions House (now known as Shields House). The old Yorktown Custom House is owned by the Comte de Grasse chapter of the National Society of the Daughters of the American Revolution. Grace Church has been restored and is an active Episcopal church. (Many of these properties are open to the public at various times of the year.)

On August 10, 1933, the U.S. War Department transferred the Yorktown National Cemetery to the National Park Service. Now enclosed by a brick wall, the two-acre cemetery is located between the Revolutionary War Yorktown Battlefield's First and Second Siege Lines.

At the corner of the cemetery is a two-story house designed by Quartermaster General Montgomery C. Meigs and built in 1866 when the national cemetery was established. For many years, the park superintendent used the home with its distinctive mansard roof. An unidentified writer from *Frank Leslie's Illustrated Newspaper* visited Yorktown in 1879 and reported that the cemetery "is admirably kept by Mr. [Mathew] Scheran(z), an ex-Federal." The story indicates that Scheranz had built a small church in the area "in return for the Samaritan services rendered to him by a Confederate soldier on the field at Gettysburg."

More recently, the cemetery is still maintained by two volunteers, Robert Reddy and Seth Pilgrim. "We perform curator-type functions," Reddy explained, such as cutting grass and cleaning out shrubbery. When they are there, the volunteers also find themselves answering questions from visitors. "People don't realize that this is a Civil War cemetery, they think it contains graves from the [Revolutionary War] siege of Yorktown," Reddy explained. "They also don't know much about the Civil War and the Peninsula Campaign" in which Yorktown was a major player.

Records indicate that 2,183 burials are identified, including known Civil War soldiers—11 Union officers, 716 white soldiers, 4 sailors, 6 African

A Union soldier reenactor poses at the Yorktown National Cemetery on Memorial Day, 2009. *Photo by Christopher Holcombe, Sons of Union Veterans, Department of Maryland.*

American soldiers and 8 known citizens. Unknown bodies include 1,412 white soldiers, 5 African American soldiers and 6 citizens. Also included are 10 unknown Confederate soldiers and 3 wives.

Not all these bodies were victims of the Yorktown siege of April and early May 1862. A number of Union veterans were moved from other sites in James City and York Counties, Williamsburg and other locations within a distance of fifty miles. The cemetery has been closed for further burials for a number of years.

Probably the most interesting grave within the cemetery is that of Private William Scott of Groton, Vermont, termed by historians as the "Sleeping Sentinel." He was a member of Company K, Third Vermont Infantry (volunteers), a group of militiamen who joined the Union army in the spring of 1861.

While at the Chain Bridge outside Washington, D.C., on August 31, 1861, Scott was found sleeping while on duty, an act that led to a court-martial and subsequent death sentence for the Union private. In his defense, Scott reportedly was exhausted and volunteered to take a sentinel place of an equally tired comrade. The commander of Scott's company, along with other offers of the brigade and regiment and many other soldiers, appealed for his life to be spared; a petition carried 191 signatures asking for leniency. President Lincoln subsequently pardoned Scott on September 8, 1861, the day before he was to be executed.

Scott returned to active duty with his unit and ultimately was killed at the Battle of Lee's Mill on April 17, 1862. It is said that he led a charge of Union soldiers against Confederate "rifle pits"—an extremely hazardous mission. His fellow soldiers remembered him as "a brave and diligent man," according to records of the New England Historical Society. He was initially buried in a grove of wild cherry and holly trees on the Garrow Farm in Warwick County (now Newport News) near the battle site. He ultimately was reinterred at the Yorktown National Cemetery.

In October 2003, Hurricane Isabel dramatically hit Virginia's Tidewater area, including Yorktown. Park rangers inspected the Yorktown National Cemetery and discovered more than a dozen trees uprooted, causing damage to about fifteen graves of Civil War–era soldiers, including the opening of shallow graves and rearranging of headstones. Apparently, grave robbers following the storm had visited the site with metal detectors, looking for historical artifacts, including uniform buttons. The park service helped repair the damaged individual graves and the graveyard.

Private William Scott of Vermont, known as the "Sleeping Sentinel," is buried in the Yorktown National Cemetery after he was killed at the nearby Battle of Lee's Mill. *Courtesy of the Vermont Historical Society.*

Six Union soldiers were reburied on May 30, 2004, in a small ceremony with honor guards from several reenactment units on hand to provide a volley salute and to play "Taps." Their bones had been scattered earlier by uprooted trees and grave robbers.

For many years, maintenance of the national cemetery has been carried out by volunteers who make sure everything is in order, especially at national holidays like Memorial Day, July 4 and Veterans Day.

17

1931 SESQUICENTENNIAL FESTIVITIES

The community of Yorktown in 1930 was viewed as "a small hamlet of few houses…[and] was without water or sewage facilities, without [street] lights, without adequate wharves," with just one improved roadway leading into and out of the town. It was ill suited for a national celebration—the 150th anniversary of the Battle of Yorktown—to be held in such an inhospitable setting, a congressional report concluded.

As in 1881, when the centennial celebration of the massive battle was held, the town had not changed much. After the one-hundredth-anniversary event, Yorktown slipped back into its quiet surroundings; all the temporary facilities were gone. Now much work needed to be accomplished, and the United States Yorktown Sesquicentennial Commission was tasked to create the program. Ultimately, it would be the most ambitious event ever held in a National Park Service area, writes Jim Burnett, former chief ranger at the Colonial National Historical Park, in his book *Hey, Ranger*.

The sesquicentennial—October 16–20, 1931—would be staged amid the turmoil of the expanding Great Depression. Nevertheless, the federal government was determined to celebrate the event. Participants included President Herbert Hoover; General of the Armies John J. Pershing, commander of American forces in World War I; and the principal French representative, Marshal Henri Pétain, commander of the French forces in the last year of World War I. Governors of the thirteen original states also attended and gave speeches.

An aerial view of the Sesquicentennial Celebration site with grandstands at right. Slabtown is located above the grounds. *National Park Service, Colonial National Historical Park.*

The main entranceway of the 1931 Sesquicentennial Celebration with exhibition tents on either side. *Special Collections Research Center, Swem Library, College of William and Mary.*

The necessary utility systems, including telephones and lights, were installed in the village with appropriate lines laid to a three-hundred-acre celebration site purchased by the federal government nearby. Finally, the area was landscaped and decorated. New roads were built, and older ones, including some pathways, were improved, Burnett explains.

In addition to the physical changes required, two other major challenges needed to be addressed: how to feed and how to house tens of thousands of expected visitors as well as the 2,500 army troops and hundreds of civilians assigned to the event. Officials decided to erect an enormous temporary tent city: one area to house overnight military and celebration personnel and another tented section for exhibits—a Colonial Fair and Harvest Festival—and space for food service.

A Richmond, Virginia restaurateur, W.E. Cease, won the competitive bid to serve food and beverages, and the army provided tents. One large tent unit contained 83,200 square feet of floor space divided into a kitchen and three dining rooms, Burnett explains. One dining room, seating 1,800 persons, was set aside for official luncheons, as on October 19, when President Hoover,

This "tent city" was erected on the battlefield for soldiers participating in the Yorktown Sesquicentennial. *From* The Yorktown Book.

The U.S. Army erected tents for exhibition space and food-service facilities. *From* The Yorktown Book.

the guest of honor, received after lunch an honorary degree from the College of William and Mary along with Pershing and Pétain. A restaurant for the public seated 800, and a cafeteria accommodated another 1,800 persons per hour. Another tent unit provided kitchen storage and covered 22,400 square feet and was equipped to hold 160,000 pounds of food. According to the army, plans were scheduled so food deliveries, by trucks under escort, arrived before dawn to avoid transportation problems.

The other problem was housing. Where would the visitors sleep? The area within a one-hundred-mile radius was canvassed to identify available rooms in hotels, boardinghouses and private homes; visitors making inquiries were given locations of possible rooms. Private vessels and steamships anchored in the York River also provided accommodations.

A grandstand was erected on the battlefield where various speeches, pageants and programs were presented. The stands provided 16,382 free seats and 7,869 paid reserved seats. Another 10,000 seats were available in adjacent bleachers. The main stage, fronting the grandstand, was eighty-five feet in diameter and included a forty-foot revolving center with an elevator that could be lowered into a pit when scenery was changed or another program readied. The grandstand and stage were used during all four days of programs.

The various pageants were extensive and elaborate, with more than 3,800 people involved. On October 19, at the very hour of the 150th anniversary surrender, a reenactment was staged for the huge crowd,

President Herbert Hoover (*center*) received an honorary degree from the College of William and Mary after an October 19 luncheon at Yorktown. *From the author's collection.*

which included the president, cabinet officials and foreign and military guests. Additionally, on that Victory Day after Hoover's speech, there was a military parade with more than 10,000 soldiers and sailors passing in review.

Both CBS and NBC radio covered the four-day festivities. The commission reported that the networks set up "very elaborate equipment for broadcasting a larger number of programs than had ever been attempted outside of Washington."

Visitors enjoyed not only the programs on the battlefield but also the naval activity on the York River. Records indicate that forty-one vessels, including a battleship, the USS *Arkansas*; one aircraft carrier, the USS *Langley*; five heavy cruisers; eight light cruisers; and seventeen destroyers were anchored offshore along with a dozen Coast Guard vessels and two French navy cruisers. Also on hand was the USS *Constitution*, the wooden-hulled, three-masted heavy frigate launched in 1797 and named by President George Washington. One of the navy's first six frigates, the ship gained its nickname "Old Ironsides" from success during the War of 1812.

Ranger Burnett explained that there were two incidents at Yorktown— one good and one bad—that have lived in sesquicentennial history. In those days, commemorative postage stamps honoring major events were collected. The two-cent Yorktown Sesquicentennial C commemorative, red and white with black portraits of Washington, Comte de Rochambeau and Comte de Grasse, was a success, with 221,037 sold at the Yorktown Post Office on the first day of issue. Ultimately, more than 1,500,000 of the stamps were sold at Yorktown.

The other was the naval salute to President Hoover planned when he arrived aboard the USS *Arizona* in Yorktown. Burnett explains that the twenty-one-gun salute was marked "by almost thirty of the naval and Coast Guard vessels present. That must have been a spectacular tribute, but one which also had the unfortunate result of breaking a number of windows in town. This [was] a good example of the 'Oops Factor'

A two-cent U.S. postal stamp was issued for the sesquicentennial and sold about 1.5 million copies at Yorktown. *From the author's collection.*

Washington's Colonials participate in the Surrender Pageant on the battlefield. *From* The Yorktown Book.

(Outcome Outside of Planned Scenario), and to the best of my knowledge, battleships or similar vessels weren't invited to fire their large guns at other subsequent events in Yorktown."

Like the 1881 centennial, this event was divided into four days of programs: October 16 was Colonial Day, October 17 Revolutionary Day, October 18 Religious Day and October 19 Victory Day. More than 200,000 people attended the events.

A related event occurred in Williamsburg on October 18. General Pershing and Marshal Pétain went to the College of William and Mary to speak and honor the French troops at the college and city before and after the battle. Pétain dedicated a memorial tablet honoring those "French Soldiers who died in Williamsburg from wounds received during the siege of Yorktown." The tablet rests on the wall of the rear portico of the Sir Christopher Wren Building on the college's eighteenth-century campus.

Historian Douglas Southall Freeman, editor of the Richmond *News Leader* newspaper, wrote, "the victory at Yorktown, to the patriots, was answered prayer, rewarded patience, vindicated faith…[and] wheresoever men read history, Yorktown symbolized the inspiring truth that resolution works revolution." And of the autumn events, Freeman acknowledged, many citizens came to Yorktown "to perform a duty rather than to learn a lesson, to see history portrayed, rather than made…[but found] something reassuring in contact with the scenes of so much faith and courage."

18

FERRYBOATS AND THE BRIDGE

From the earliest colonial days, the narrows of the York River between the Port of York on the south side and Tyndall's Point on the north needed to be bridged for effective transportation and communication. Indians used canoes for centuries to traverse the mile-wide water.

By the mid-1600s, the colonists sought ways to span eastern Virginia's rivers and streams. A ferry quickly became the preferred mode of travel. By the early nineteenth century, there were more than one hundred ferries operating throughout Virginia.

In 1641, the House of Burgesses established Virginia's first laws regarding ferries. It decreed that each county was responsible for providing and maintaining ferries and bridges at needed points.

For the next three-hundred-plus years, a ferryboat operated from Yorktown to Tyndall's Point (now Gloucester Point). Sailing vessels and, later, steamboats augmented the ferryboats on the York, but it was not until 1952 and the construction of the George Preston Coleman Memorial Bridge that the linkage ran above the water rather than through it.

It is believed that a ferry was authorized in York County about 1647 at a point not far from where the Port of York would be established later in the century. Initially, it was a poled or rowed ferry that operated intermittently for about fifty years.

In March 1654, the law provided that the counties could license ferry-keepers. Robert Reed, justice of the peace for York County, on March 24, 1694, granted Colonel Thomas Pate III of Gloucester County a license to

This is a late nineteenth-century polled ferry, the type used for many years between Yorktown and Gloucester Point. *Special Collections Research Center, Swem Library, College of William and Mary.*

operate a ferry and "keep an ordinary" at the Port of York. On January 24, 1699, York County renewed the license for Pate to maintain an ordinary "as he had been doing [and] to keep a ferry near Yorktown at the usual place commonly called by the name of the well 'where the ships usually watered.'"

In 1702, the House of Burgesses reissued the license to "keep the Ferry at York Town" to Pate and Mungo Somerwell. Pate died in 1703, and the ferry apparently did not operate for two years until the House of Burgesses reestablished it in 1705.

Ferry service operated by individuals continued at Yorktown through the eighteenth century. After the poles, large oars were used to row across the river; much later, cables were used. Ferry traffic was especially heavy as the port grew with the increased production of tobacco in the region. Similar activity was generated across the river at Gloucester Point (formerly Tyndall's Point).

The April 14, 1774 edition of the *Virginia Gazette* carries a notice from Janet Mitchell and Mary Gibbons of Yorktown, managers of the ferry. Effective April 1, the women advised, "Gentlemen who cross to pay their

Ferriages at the Swan Tavern," and they assured customers that "the Ferry shall be kept inferior to none in the Colony."

The lone mention of ferries during the Battle of Yorktown came in the description of General Charles, Lord Cornwallis's, attempt "to ferry" his troops across the river to Gloucester from where they hoped to escape. Cornwallis was going to move his troops using his own ships and probably not the private ferry.

By the early nineteenth century, the ferry was using a cable rather than oars to make the crossing. Within a few years, steamboats began to supplement the river's transportation and communication, but unfortunately, rarely just went from Yorktown to Gloucester. The boats systematically provided regular steamboat service along the entire York River from the Chesapeake Bay to the town of West Point upriver from Yorktown. In addition to their commercial and passenger routes, the steamboats, in the summertime, frequently offered leisure trips, including all-day excursions.

The ferry service became very irregular during the Civil War; what boats operated were privately owned. Records indicate that on March 6, 1886, the Virginia General Assembly formally authorized William H. Ash of Gloucester to operate a ferry between Yorktown and Gloucester Point. The bill acknowledged that Ash had been operating previously under an act of the House of Burgesses at least 120 years old. There had been a challenge that the old act probably became ineffective when the ferry service was discontinued during the Civil War. Ash was allowed to run the ferry under rates adopted in 1867 by the Gloucester County Court.

In 1918, a subsequent member of the Ash family, William T. Ash, had a ferry constructed large enough to carry numerous automobiles. Caroline C. Brooks, writing in *Chesapeake Style* magazine, remembers her first ride on the Gloucester-Yorktown Ferry in her "granddaddy Richardson's Model T Ford." On the boat, "I loved to climb the stairs" up to the restrooms and pilothouse. On another ride, she was in a Nash coupe that had a rumble seat. "I rode in the rumble seat rain or shine. When it rained I used a waterproof coat that protected me" even on the ferry ride.

Many years ago, the late Katherine Jordan Fenstermacher of Gloucester recalled that, in the early twentieth century, the Gloucester-Yorktown Ferry had a one-horsepower engine that operated a small flattop boat that carried a horse and buggy and pedestrians across the river. The first "real ferry," she said, was the enclosed *Cornwallis*; others were the *Palmetto*, *Miss Gloucester*, *York*, *Miss Washington* and *Virginia*. The *Cornwallis* was purchased in 1919.

This is typical of the rope ferry used from the middle of the nineteenth century at Yorktown. This photograph was taken in 1900 on the Yadkin River in North Carolina. *Courtesy of the State Archives of North Carolina.*

The first enclosed ferry between Yorktown and Gloucester Point was the *Cornwallis*, purchased in 1919. *Special Collections Research Center, Swem Library, College of William and Mary.*

The *Automobile Blue Book of 1923*, the forerunner of the AAA Travel Guide, provides all the information any traveler needed when using U.S. Highway 17 through Gloucester down to the ferry. Times and fees are specifically listed.

As with all boats, there were ferry accidents. The great hurricane of August 23, 1933, caused many problems for the Gloucester-Yorktown Ferry. Accompanying the high winds throughout the area, the tides ran significantly high. The eye of the storm crossed Norfolk and then moved very near the York River narrows. Fenstermacher said the wind and waves destroyed the steamboat dock at Yorktown along with the side-slip for the extra ferry, *The Palmetto*. The other operating ferry rode out the storm in the middle of the river.

Two accidents occurred in 1943, she recalled. In January, a bus was the last vehicle to board the ferry at Gloucester during an unusual high tide. The bus's bumper got caught in the landing ramp of the dock, and the bus fell into the river when the ferry pulled out. Several days later, there was another bus accident, this time with the first vehicle to board. When the brakes failed, the bus immediately plunged nose-first into the river. No one was injured in either accident.

In the 1940s, a one-way trip on the ferry for car and driver was fifty-five cents, with eighty cents for a round-trip. Walk-on passengers and other car passengers paid fifteen cents each.

As the years passed, larger ferryboats were built and began their journeys across the York River. *From the collection of Richard Shisler, Yorktown, Virginia.*

The last ferryboat added to the York River fleet was the *Virginia*. Built in 1936 as the *City of Burlington* for the Lake Champlain ferry service, the twenty-five-car vessel was moved to Virginia in 1942 and renamed the *Virginia*. It ran the last Gloucester-Yorktown crossing at noon on May 7, 1952. Captain Sam Belvin of Gloucester was her captain. (The *Virginia* then was transferred to the Jamestown-Surry Ferry Fleet on the James River and was finally retired in 2018.)

Highway traffic dramatically increased after World War II, and the Virginia Department of Highways determined that a bridge was necessary over the York between York and Gloucester Counties. The Coleman Bridge, a two-lane, 3,750-foot-long double-swing span connection opened on May 7, 1952, replacing the long-running ferry.

Virginia governor John S. Battle formally opened the bridge by riding across it in his convertible limousine. Then he was driven down to the old dock and made the last ferry ride from Gloucester Point to Yorktown. The bridge was named for George Preston Coleman, commissioner (agency head) of the Virginia Department of Highways from 1913 to 1922. When constructed,

On May 7, 1952, the Yorktown-Gloucester Ferry made its last run and the George Preston Coleman Memorial Bridge opened. This scene shows the last ferry (*center left*) coming into the Yorktown dock; the new bridge has already opened. *Courtesy of Jim Krikales, Yorktown, Virginia.*

it was the world's largest double-swing-span bridge. Today, it ranks second. The bridge engineers were Parsons Brinckerhoff, Inc. The firm, in 1957, also designed the Hampton Roads Bridge-Tunnel connecting the Phoebus section of Hampton with the Willoughby Spit area of Norfolk, Virginia.

An interesting by-product of the building of the bridge was that the Virginia Fisheries Laboratory located on the beach at Yorktown had to be moved. Subsequently, the lab was relocated across the river at Gloucester Point on a large campus and became the Virginia Institute of Marine Science, now part of the College of William and Mary.

The Coleman Bridge initially cost more than $9 million, and the double-swing span was needed to accommodate ships traveling upstream to several military installations in the region, primarily the U.S. Naval Weapons Station Yorktown. At the highest point, the bridge is about 90 feet above the York, where the river's natural depth is 60 feet. The horizontal navigational clearance is 450 feet.

In 1994, the Virginia Department of Transportation began a massive project to expand the bridge from two to four lanes because vehicle use of

In 1995, the Coleman Bridge was expanded from two lanes to four. Here, one of the sections on a barge is readied for placement. *Virginia Department of Transportation, photo by Alvin Alston.*

A U.S. Navy ship has left the Yorktown Naval Weapons Station upstream and is getting ready to sail under the Coleman Bridge. *U.S. Navy photo.*

The George Preston Coleman Memorial Bridge has been in operation since 1952 and was enlarged in 1995. *Courtesy of York County.*

the bridge was exceeding 27,000 per day. The project required widening the two approaches and reworking and heavily reinforcing the concrete pier caps on each of the bridge's pillars across the river.

The old bridge was dismantled, and the new bridge with its wider roadway was put into place between May 4 and May 13, 1995. The new bridge's 2,500 feet of truss and swing spans were floated forty miles up the York River from Norfolk, where they had been fabricated. The cost of the reconstructed Coleman Bridge was about $97 million, including engineering and construction. The original toll on the old bridge had been eliminated in 1976. However, a toll was reinstated in 1995 to help pay for the new structure. The new fee is $2 per two-axle vehicle (northbound only).

19

NICK AND MARY MATHEWS

Nick's Seafood Pavilion

When someone was asked where was the best place to eat in Yorktown, Virginia, the answer was quick and simple: "Nick's Seafood Pavilion." Why was that? Again, another quick answer: "Nick and Mary Mathews, the owners!"

Greek immigrants Nikolaos Matheos of Karpathos and Mary Pappamihalopoulou of Sparta were married in New York and moved to Virginia in 1944. They were lovers of America and lovers of Yorktown. They were fervent patriots who constantly promoted the red, white and blue.

Through the years, their generosity to the military was boundless. "No one in uniform who came to the restaurant had to pay—it was free of charge at Nick's," explained Jim Krikales, an employee at Nick's for forty years, the last eighteen as general manager until he retired in 2001.

The restaurant the Matheweses built became known the world over. Visitors came by the thousands to enjoy the excellent seafood and the artistic decor of the building that ultimately was expanded three times and could seat four-hundred-plus people. It was not unusual for patrons to stand in line for an hour. Governors, U.S. senators, state officials and actors like John Wayne and Elizabeth Taylor, singer Tony Bennett and a host of other entertainers came to Nick's.

Mary Mathews collected paintings and statues to put in the restaurant. "Mary would hear about an antique store going out of business and would go there and buy everything—all the paintings, sculptures and artwork,"

Nick and Mary Mathews stand in a dining room of their restaurant—Nick's Seafood Pavilion. *Courtesy of the Jamestown-Yorktown Foundation.*

explained Krikales, whose wife, Ann, started working at the restaurant in 1954, seven years before he did.

Subsequently, the building's decor, including a half dozen Nubian statues and massive crystal chandeliers, became attractions in themselves. One writer described the decorations as "over-the-top gaudiness" but admitted that, to its fans, "it was one of its main attributes."

"Mister Nick," as he was called, and "Miss Mary" often spoke of Yorktown as "the beginning of our freedom." About 1970, on the eve of the nation's bicentennial celebration, the Mathewses played an invaluable role in connection with the Virginia Independence Bicentennial Commission's Yorktown Victory Center. The center was designed to explain the scenario of the American Revolution leading up to and including the Battle of Yorktown. It was not simply a museum; instead, it was to enhance and supplement the existing attractions—the Park Service Visitors Center, the colonial buildings and battlefield.

Numerous sites were explored, and the commission concluded that the center would be built in adjoining Newport News. But Nick and Mary disagreed. The center, they contended, needed to be at Yorktown. They

The interior of Nick's Seafood Pavilion was its own attraction, with paintings and artwork as seen in this postcard. *From the author's collection.*

offered a gift of twenty-five acres of battlefield land overlooking the river, but the state did not readily accept the property. The Mathewses traveled to the Virginia General Assembly in Richmond in 1972 to convince the legislators to take their donation. Eventually, the land, valued at between $500,000 and $700,000, became state property, and the Victory Center was designed, constructed and opened in 1976.

When the center was dedicated, a plaque read: "This bicentennial memorial honoring the victory at Yorktown is offered as a lasting symbol of patriotism and gratitude by Dr. Nicholas and Mary Mathews. To you from failing hands we pass the torch. Be it yours and hold it high."

There is a great story about the Victory Center property, Krikales explained. "Some years before, a group of businessmen came into the restaurant and talked with Nick about buying the property. They wanted to build a hotel. He said, 'no,' and they upped the price. Finally, they offered about $700,000, and he still refused to sell. 'What are you going to do with that land?' they asked. 'Well, he said, maybe I'll go up there and hunt deer.'" Krikales said Nick went back into the kitchen. "They said, 'he's crazy,' then just got up and left."

The Mathewses' Yorktown saga began with a visit to Mary's sister, who lived in the town; the New York couple became enchanted with the community and decided to move south and open a restaurant. "Nick found a site he wanted and made the owner an offer he couldn't refuse," Krikales recalled. "He opened the Seashore Pavilion, where they remained until he erected a new building that became Nick's Seafood Pavilion."

They worked eighteen to twenty hours a day. Nick was waiter, chef and dishwasher; Mary handled everything out front. Their first eatery was little more than a café with about thirty seats. The menu in August 1945 offered crab chowder for $0.20, fried sea trout and "selected oysters" for $0.70 each. In 1957, a lobster tail cost $3.00.

About 1952, the Mathewses constructed a restaurant with a larger dining room on adjoining property, and Nick's began to take off. A second dining room was added in 1957, and they built a new lobby in 1961. A third dining room in the rear—the Nile Room—with a running water feature was also constructed in 1961.

Ann Krikales, who worked for many years at Nick's alongside her husband, agreed that the most popular menu items were seafood shish kebab, lobster Dien Bien rice and broiled whole flounder. Baked Alaska was tops on the desert menu, and everyone enjoyed the large salads with Greek dressing.

Mr. Nick told the *Washington Post* many years ago that seafood shish kebab "was my creation. I thought it up [in the early 1970s]. It has shrimp, scallops,

Nick and Mary Mathews opened the Seashore Pavilion in 1945. *Courtesy of Jim Krikales.*

The Seashore Pavilion was a very small café that very soon, because of its food, began to attract notice. *Courtesy of York County Parks, Recreation & Tourism.*

lobster, onion, tomato, mushrooms—all cooked in real butter....They talk about it all the way to California." With good food and large portions, Nick's continued to prosper. "We always got seafood fresh, even delivered on the weekend," Krikales explained. "Nick said they pay for meals, give them a little extra."

The nation, Virginia and Yorktown celebrated the bicentennial of the Battle of Yorktown and subsequent British surrender in October 1981 with a multiday program and appearances by U.S. president Ronald Reagan and French president Francois Mitterrand. The Mathewses were involved in numerous ways, but most important, they spent about $180,000 in 1981 to erect a memorial on their waterfront property across the street from the restaurant. Included were plaques honoring the U.S. presidents born in Virginia and the three presidents—Chester A. Arthur, Herbert Hoover and Reagan—who participated in the 1881, 1931 and 1981 Yorktown commemorations, respectively. Years later, with the riverfront renovation, the plaques from the monument were moved elsewhere in the town.

Mary and Nick Mathews received numerous tributes and honors, including honorary doctorates from Christopher Newport University in Newport News. A special recognition came in 1983 when the U.S. Navy

Ann and Jim Krikales were employees and good friends of Nick and Mary Mathews's. They worked at Nick's Seafood Pavilion for more than three decades. *Courtesy of Ann and Jim Krikales.*

named Mary the sponsor of the new USS *Yorktown*, an Aegis guided-missile cruiser that was to be launched in Pascagoula, Mississippi. The Krikaleses joined the Mathewses for the navy airplane trip to the christening program on April 14, 1983. During the flight, Nick died of a heart attack. Although grief-stricken, Mary asked for the agenda to continue; she participated in all the activities, including the christening on April 17.

With Mr. Nick's death, Miss Mary continued to operate the restaurant. Whenever the USS *Yorktown* came up the York River and passed the restaurant, she would run outside and wave an American flag. She was recognized for her contributions to the new gallery at the Victory Center on April 11, 1995, when former president George H.W. Bush spoke at the ceremony.

Near the end of her life, Mary was concerned about York County's redevelopment project along the waterfront and thought the proposed restrooms on the beach were a "disgrace." A member of the Yorktown Trustees, a group of five citizens appointed by the court to manage the "common-land" along the shoreline of the town for more than 250 years, she often opposed anything that would change the face of her community and was a frequent discomfort to her fellow trustees. (The Virginia General Assembly abolished the trustees in 2003, with their authority passing to York County.)

When she died on September 23, 1998, at age eighty-two, Miss Mary was buried alongside Mr. Nick in a large marble tomb on a knoll near the

Nick's Seafood Pavilion stood on the Yorktown waterfront for fifty years. *From the author's collection.*

Victory Center. During her funeral, the American flag was draped over her casket, just as it was done for Nick years earlier. Mary left the restaurant and thirteen parcels of land in Yorktown to the Jamestown-Yorktown Foundation Trust, a fundraising and development arm of the Jamestown-Yorktown Foundation, the Virginia state agency that ran the Victory Center. In 2001, the trust sold the property and restaurant to York County for $3 million; the revenue was to be used for programs at the Victory Center.

Hurricane Isabel with its drastic storm surge struck eastern Virginia on September 18, 2003, and effectively closed Nick's Seafood Pavilion. York County planned to shutter the old building by the end of the year as part of its waterfront improvement program. But Isabel brought sudden death, flooding the building.

In a way completing the "full circle," Krikales became a partner and chef in 2005 at the River Room of the Duke of York Hotel, about two blocks down Water Street from where Nick's restaurant stood. There he offered patrons many of the favorite dishes from Nick's menu. Krikales finally retired in 2014.

Twenty years after Miss Mary's passing and thirty-five after Mr. Nick's death, the couple is still remembered by Yorktown citizens as well as the Commonwealth of Virginia. On April 1, 2017, the new American Revolution Museum at Yorktown, which replaced the worn-out Victory Center, was dedicated to the memory of Nick and Mary Mathews. A plaque on the brick wall near the entrance to the museum dedicated to the Mathewses says it all: "Their generosity and passionate love for the United Sates defined their lives."

20

BICENTENNIAL CELEBRATION
OF 1981

Ronald Reagan and François Mitterrand stood side by side on October 19, 1981, to review several thousand participants, many clad in colonial-era uniforms, parading as the troops might have done on Surrender Field at Yorktown two hundred years earlier.

A two-hour ceremony, dramatically splashed with the colors of history, brought the two presidents together to publicly reaffirm the long-lasting French and American friendship forged here in 1781. There were three major addresses and a gathering of modern-day military and colonial reenactor troops saluting and honoring the alliance. This field had not seen such pageantry in fifty years, since the 1931 sesquicentennial celebration of the surrender on October 19, 1781, of British general Charles, Lord Cornwallis.

The two presidents spoke, but it was the British representative—Quintin Hogg, Lord Hailsham, lord chancellor of England and speaker of the House of Lords—whose spirited evocation sounded the day's theme. Unlike the 1881 centennial and 1931 sesquicentennial events, when no British envoys were invited, Lord Hailsham was asked to be part of the official party. The third of the main speakers, he proclaimed, "Nothing [is] quite so humbling for those with responsibility for the present as the contemplation of the past." It is important, he added, for the three nations to come together now "to reflect for a moment on the lessons of history" and also "ponder the future, too."

The Victory Day program was held in a battlefield stadium erected with bleachers and a large, enclosed, bright-blue reviewing stand with a

U.S. president Ronald Reagan (*right*) and French president François Mitterrand pose just before the October 19, 1981 Bicentennial Celebration at Yorktown. *Courtesy of the Ronald Reason Library.*

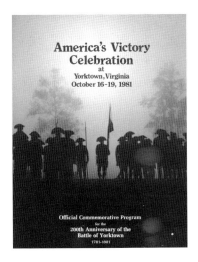

America's Victory
Celebration
at
Yorktown, Virginia
October 16-19, 1981

Official Commemorative Program
for the
200th Anniversary of the
Battle of Yorktown
1781-1981

The official program of the 200th anniversary of the Battle of Yorktown. *Special Collections Research Center, Swem Library, College of William and Mary.*

bulletproof screen protecting Mitterrand and Reagan, who had been injured in an assassination attempt seven months earlier.

The audience of about sixty thousand was treated to an eye-catching spectacle—a military review—featuring more than five thousand troops, including about nine hundred cadets fro... the Virginia Military Institute, as well as formal French, German and British twentieth-century military units accompanied by the Colonial and British reenactors who appeared on program segments throughout the celebration.

As a sidebar to the celebration, it should be noted that American-French relations had been somewhat strained, and the meeting at Yorktown between the two presidents was the important beginning of many face-to-face sessions held throughout the remainder of Reagan's presidency. In addition to their battlefield appearance, earlier gatherings came the day before with a luncheon aboard the French ship *Comte de Grasse* in the York River and an elaborate evening banquet at the reconstructed Governor's Palace at Colonial Williamsburg.

The Virginia Independence Bicentennial Commission (VIBC) (1966–82) was created by the Virginia General Assembly and staffed to manage the statewide commemoration of the independence of the United States. In 1976, Virginia opened three major visitor centers designed as focal points for the numerous historical attractions planned for the bicentennial. Located in Alexandria, Charlottesville and Yorktown, the centers focused on special events planned from 1976 through 1981 in counties, towns and cities from the mountains to the sea, with Yorktown as the climactic event.

Unlike the 1881 and 1931 celebrations, there was no federal commission established to help direct the programs. Therefore, the Yorktown Bicentennial Committee was created with personnel from the National Park Service, the VIBC, York County and Yorktown. Retired navy captain Randall Young, director of the Yorktown Victory Center, put together nearly two dozen committees eventually involving about 250 volunteers. But the Yorktown Bicentennial Committee (YBC) needed more help to ensure success.

Virginia governor John N. Dalton, at the request of the VIBC, stepped in at a critical stage and directed various state offices to take over management of the program, as it had become so involved and complicated with the number of foreign visitors and guests expected. Many of the much-needed state personnel made their offices in Yorktown weeks in advance. William B. Rowland Jr., deputy director of the Department of Planning and Budget, was appointed staff director; Albert W. Coates Jr., longtime special assistant to the commissioner of highways, served as public affairs director and press coordinator; and Trudy Norfleet, secretary to a former governor, was the group's secretary. Other members of the governor's "Yorktown Brigade," as it was called, included Mike Rogers, Elizabeth Biehn, Stan Kidwell, Dan Bartges, Al Neale and Pauline Demonds. About the same time, the VIBC named Ross L. Weeks Jr. its director.

Ultimately, the four-day event, October 16–19, was a rousing success; tens of thousands of visitors descended on Yorktown each day.

The festivities were divided into four specific programs. Friday, October 16, was Festival Day, with a parade, reenactments of the storming of the British redoubts by men portraying American and French troops. The Colonial Heritage Festival, with sixteen acres of exhibits, entertainments

Re-created colonial units were part of the military parade on October 19, 1981, at the battlefield at Yorktown. *Courtesy of the Jamestown-Yorktown Foundation.*

and refreshments, opened. There also were various period ships and demonstrations on the York River.

October 17 was designated Military Day, with a reenactment of the historic "Call for Parley," when a British drummer boy and a soldier with a white flag appeared atop a British embankment seeking a cessation of the fighting. There were speeches by military leaders and tactical demonstrations. Sunday, October 18, was Patriots' Day, with an interdenominational religious service, music and dramatic presentations and still more battle reenactments. To end the day, there was an elaborate bonfire, a *feu de jole* or rifle salute and a fireworks display. Victory Day, October 19—the surrender anniversary date—featured speeches by Reagan, Mitterrand and Lord Hailsham; the surrender reenactment; and a grand military parade.

At the Yorktown Victory Center, across town from the battlefield, one of the state's bicentennial centers, a special exhibit was mounted. Titled, *The World Turned Upside Down*, the exhibit featured all types of memorabilia, including George Washington's military trunk and diary and the "surrender table" used when the Articles of Capitulation were written. Two paintings by French artist Louis-Nicolas van Blarenberghe, *The Siege of Yorktown* and *Surrender at Yorktown*, were displayed. They were on loan from Versailles and had never before been shown in the United States.

The visitor center of the Colonial National Historical Park, located almost in the center of the celebration, had a display of military equipment used in the eighteenth century and at the Yorktown surrender, including Washington's tent.

Dozens of newspaper and television outlets descended upon Yorktown; stories encompassing nearly every aspect of the program and historical events were recounted. For example, camp life at a British reenactment unit was made realistic when a mock flogging was staged. The soldier had been charged with "improperly shining his brass buttons." The common punishment for such an offense was flogging.

At other reenactment military camps around the battlefield, there were "camp followers"—in colonial days, wives, girlfriends and even prostitutes—on hand to add to the historical representations. They even staged a small protest when they were told they could not march with their military units.

To accommodate the daily crowds, the Virginia Department of Highways (later Department of Transportation) set up an elaborate bus system to carry visitors from designated parking areas to the celebration site. Planning for the shuttle bus system began when highway officials visited Lake Placid, New York, the site of the 1980 Winter Olympics.

Colorful pageantry became part of the festivities at the 1981 Bicentennial Celebration. *Courtesy of the Jamestown-Yorktown Foundation.*

That system had collapsed on the first day, and highway personnel did not want that to happen at Yorktown. Their efforts paid off, and the Yorktown system worked well.

The 1981 event joined the history books, and research studies naturally will become a planning resource for the 2031 celebration of the 250th anniversary of the Battle of Yorktown.

21

MUSEUMS COVER TOWN'S HISTORY

The American Revolution Museum at Yorktown did more than physically replace the old Victory Center. Its new exhibits expanded visitors' appreciation and understanding of how the common man and woman shaped and were shaped by the Revolution and the founding of the new nation.

With a grand opening in March 2017, the 80,000-square-foot building cost about $50 million in state funds, with private donations supporting adjacent multi-acre outdoor living history exhibits as well as the creation of a variety of innovative displays. Situated on a small bluff overlooking the York River, the museum replaces the Yorktown Victory Center, which opened in 1976 as part of Virginia's tribute to the nation's bicentennial.

An award-winning introductory documentary film, *Liberty Fever*, is shown every thirty minutes in a 170-seat theater at the entrance to the exhibition wing. The film sets the stage for the exhibits that follow and focuses on individuals who played roles in various aspects of the Revolution. In the film, an early nineteenth-century storyteller recounts his travels through the growing new nation, gathering stories about the American Revolution. These accounts are presented through a moving panorama device—two large spool-type apparatuses that, when turned, cause the canvas to scroll. This creates an illusion of movement and becomes an unusual technique for engaging the twenty-first-century audience in an eighteenth-century story.

The theme of ordinary people is woven throughout the manifold exhibits "of the world of Revolutionary America." The permanent 22,000 square

The entryway to the new $50 million American Revolution Museum at Yorktown complex. *Courtesy of the Jamestown-Yorktown Foundation.*

feet of gallery space create a journey with artifacts, interactive exhibits, dioramas and short films from the colonial era prior to the Revolution, through the armed conflict to years of the Constitution and beyond. One reviewer wrote that "comprehensive indoor exhibits and outdoor living history capture the transformational nature and epic scale of the Revolution and its relevance today."

Nearly five hundred artifacts are on display, including an early Declaration of Independence broadside from July 1776; a coronation portrait of King George III of Great Britain; a portrait of General Charles, Lord Cornwallis, British commander at Yorktown; iron slave shackles; an antislavery Wedgwood medallion circa 1790; an American silver-hilted, eagle-pommel sword, circa 1776; a Continental Congress pamphlet of 1774; a George Washington epaulette star, circa 1799; and a portrait circa 1733, one of the earliest known, of an enslaved African in the American colonies.

A collection of portraits greets guests in the hallway that parallels the exhibition area. Among the historical characters are Isabella Ferguson, an Irish immigrant and patriot; Peter Harris, Catawba Indian and soldier;

George Hewes, witness to the Boston Massacre; and Billy Flora, African American soldier and hero of the Battle of Great Bridge near Norfolk, Virginia. These men and women proclaim, "I was there" and reappear in various situations elsewhere in the museum. Also along the wall is the exhibition timeline.

There are five major thematic areas: the British Empire and America; the Changing Relationship—Britain and North America; Revolution; the New Nation; and the American People. The Revolution area offers insight from the early days of Lexington and Concord in 1775 to the Yorktown victory.

Part of the museum's mission is to educate and provide history lessons, not just present historical facts. Interactive elements enable visitors, especially students, to work through problems or themes, often using touch-screen maps to explore subjects such as colonial America and Revolutionary War battles. One of the highlights is "The Siege of Yorktown," a 180-degree surround screen with a 4-D experience—thunder shakes the seats, smoke comes up from the floor and explosions disrupt the dialogue. The tale is well told.

The last two sections of the indoor experience relate to the forming of the United States and the creation of the Constitution and the Bill of Rights

One of the galleries of the American Revolution Museum features a statue of Patrick Henry in front of the Red Lion Tavern, where a short film explains the colonists' growing anger over British taxation. *Courtesy of the Jamestown-Yorktown Foundation.*

157

and how the nation has been influenced by immigration, demographics and political and social change.

The outdoor living history area includes a Continental army encampment and a Revolution-era farm. It contains not only a drill field but also tents for soldiers and officers and a demonstration area for artillery and rifles. At the farm, a homestead with kitchen and tobacco barn with slave quarters demonstrates life in the 1750s, most likely in Virginia. During various seasons, crop fields, kitchen gardens and orchard will flourish.

The museum is open daily except Christmas and New Year's Days, and an entry fee is charged.

Down the bluff and nearly under the George P. Coleman Memorial Bridge and located on Water Street is another important Yorktown museum—the Watermen's Museum. A niche museum and not widely known, it is dedicated to preserving the heritage of the watermen of the Chesapeake Bay and demonstrating the role of the watermen from colonial to modern times.

Through the efforts of Marian Hornsby Bowditch, whose father was a waterman and later a businessman, and Nancy Laing Cole Laurier, both longtime Yorktown residents, the museum opened in 1981 as a local contribution to the bicentennial celebration. Initially, it was just an exhibition of four rooms in small brick building on the old Yorktown waterfront. It survived but did not create much attention until 1986, when Cypress Manor, a large home across the York River in Gloucester County, became available; but it had to be moved.

Cyprus Manor, a large frame home from Gloucester County, was moved on a barge in 1987 to Yorktown and became the Watermen's Museum. *Courtesy of the Newport News* Daily Press, *photo by Joe Fudge.*

The Watermen's Museum on the shore of the York River in Yorktown. *Courtesy of Alexander Kravets, Yorktown, Virginia.*

Owners Bob and Jan Kukicki decided to donate the large frame home and three smaller outbuildings to the museum if Marian Bowditch would raise the funds for the move. Money was raised, and the house was placed on a barge and moved down the river in 1987 to its new Yorktown location, the site of the old Hornsby Oil Company storage facility and the old Gloucester-Yorktown ferry dock. The oil company was owned and operated by Marian Bowditch's father.

Between 1987 and 2017, the museum expanded its operation. The renovated home was opened in 1989 with the rooms featuring displays telling the story of the watermen in Tidewater Virginia. The outbuildings became a boat shop, storage building and events building. Also placed on the property in 2011 was a two-story representation of a three-story colonial windmill that was thought to be located on the bluff behind the museum. Built by Walt and Evelyn Akers of the Twisted Oak Foundation, it is on loan to the museum.

Visitors to the museum learn from the watermen's perspective as demonstrated through the workboat and hand tool exhibits in the home's old library. The first workboats were log canoes that were fastened together, with three or five forming a hull. Next came the bugeye, a style of sailboard developed in the Chesapeake Bay for oyster dredging. It was the predecessor of the skipjack, which, with its large sail, became the most popular boat. With the development of the diesel motor, the deadrise boat became the official vessel of Virginia watermen. The deadrise has a sharp bow that extends down the hull into a large V-shape. It has a square stern.

Another area features Lord Cornwallis's sunken fleet and the explorations and archaeological activities conducted around the old vessels since the 1800s. (See chapter 9.)

Two major historical events in the area—the Revolutionary War and the Civil War—are explained in the context of their relationships to the bay and the York River. Important in the presentation are the specific facts. For instance, there was no battle between the *Monitor* and *Merrimack*, one guide explained. To be precise, the first battle of ironclad warships was between the Union *Monitor* and the Confederate *Virginia*, which had iron armor built on the old lower hull and deck of the former Union ship *Merrimack*.

The museum is open annually from April until late fall. Hours vary, and there are often scheduled outdoor and evening programs.

The National Park Service operates another museum of importance in its visitor center adjacent to the battlefield. These exhibits focus on the siege of Yorktown and the Battle of the Capes between British and French warships. A one-quarter-scale ship reproduction of a portion of the British forty-four-gun frigate the *Charon* allows visitors to experience a section of the gun deck

The visitor center at Colonial National Historical Park features a one-quarter-scale model of a portion of the interior of a British warship. *Photo by the author.*

with its cannon and part of the captain's cabin. Also on display are the campaign table used by Cornwallis during the siege and campaign tents used by Washington.

Park rangers offer specialized, intermittent guided tours and information about the seven-mile self-drive battlefield tour. A CD is available for the seventy-five-minute tour. The visitor center and battlefield are open daily except Thanksgiving, Christmas and New Year's; grounds close daily at sunset.

The York County Historical Museum is located in the lower level of York Hall in the heart of Yorktown's historic area and in a white clapboard building on Main Street. Exhibits range from artifacts associated with Native American, Colonial, Revolutionary and Civil War eras to the USS *Yorktown*, the old battlefield golf course and the nearby naval weapons station. Open days and hours vary for the county museum.

SELECTED BIBLIOGRAPHY

Acomb, Evelyn M., ed. "The Revolutionary Journal of Baron Ludwig von Closen, 1780–1783." Williamsburg, VA: Omohundro Institute of Earl American History and Culture and the University of North Carolina Press, 2012.

Bailey, Ronald H. *The Civil War: Forward to Richmond*. Alexandria, VA: Time-Life Books, 1983.

Barka, Norman F., Edward Ayres and Christine Sheridan. "The 'Poor Potter' of Yorktown: A Study of a Colonial Pottery Factory, Colonial National Historical Park." Denver: United States Department of Interior, National Park Service.

Behrend, Jackie Eileen. *The Hauntings of Williamsburg, Yorktown and Jamestown*. Winston-Salem, NC: John F. Blair, 1998.

Campbell, Charles. "Jamestown, Williamsburg and Yorktown." *Southern Literary Messenger*, April 1837.

Clark, Frances Watson. *The Colonial Parkway*. Charleston, SC: Arcadia Publishing, 2010.

"Colonial National Historical Park, Virginia." Washington, DC: U.S. Government Printing Office, 1940.

Deetz, Kelly. "Slabtown: Yorktown's African American Community, 1863–1970." Senior honors thesis, College of William and Mary, 2002.

Dill, Alonzo Thomas. *York River Yesterdays*. Norfolk/Virginia Beach, VA: Donning Company, 1993.

Erickson, Mark St. John. "A Cradle of Slavery on the York." *Daily Press*, May 25, 2013.

———. "DAR Preserved Yorktown History with 'A Lot of Stamina and Faith.'" *Daily Press (Newport News)*, May 8, 2013.

———. "Historic Black Church Rises from the Yorktown Contraband Camp." *Daily Press*, April 29, 2013.

———. "Lost Black Township in York County Lives On in Memory." *Daily Press*, February 22, 2016.

———. "Remembering the Surrender at Yorktown." *Daily Press*, October 19, 2013.

Evans, Charles M. *The War of the Aeronauts: A History of Ballooning During the Civil War*. Mechanicsburg, PA, 2002.

Ferguson, Homer L. "Salvaging Revolutionary Relics from the York River." *William and Mary Quarterly Historical Magazine* 19, no. 3, July 1939.

Frisinger, Kerrie. "Civil War Graves Too Damaged, Too." *Daily Press*, October 10, 2003.

Harper's Weekly, Journal of Civilization, October 22, 1881, October 29, 1881.

Hatch, Charles E., Jr. "Storehouse and Customhouse." *Virginia Cavalcade* XVI, no. 2 (Autumn 1966).

Holmes, Reverend Richard John. *History of Shiloh Baptist Church*. Yorktown, VA: Shiloh Baptist Church, 1974.

Holmes, Richard. *Falling Upwards: How We Took to the Air*. New York: Pantheon, 2013.

Howe, Henry. *Historical Collections of Virginia*. Charleston, SC: Babcock & Company, 1845.

Jackson, Luther Porter. *Negro Office-holders in Virginia, 1865–1895*. Norfolk, VA: Guide Quality Press, 1945.

Johnston, Henry P. *The Yorktown Campaign and the Surrender of Cornwallis*. New York: Harper & Brothers, 1881.

Lossing, Benson John. *Pictorial Field-Book of The Revolution*. New York: Harper & Brothers, 1855.

Lowe, T.S.C. *Memoirs of Thaddeus S.C. Lowe, Chief of the Aeronautic Corps of the Army of the United States During the Civil War: My Balloons in Peace and War*. Lewiston, NY: Edwin Mellen Press, 2004.

Manley, Kathleen. *A History of Yorktown and Its Victory Celebrations—Revival to Patriotism*. Charleston, SC: The History Press, 2005.

———. Images of America: *Yorktown*. Charleston, SC: Arcadia Publishing, 2004.

Manley, Kathleen, and Richard Shisler. Postcard History Series: *Yorktown*. Charleston, SC: Arcadia Publishing, 2017.

Mcllwaine, Henry Read, ed. "Journal of the House of Burgesses, 1702/3–1705, 1705–1706, 1710–1712." Richmond: Virginia State Library Board, 1912.

Middleton, Arthur Pierce. *Tobacco Coast: A Maritime History of Chesapeake Bay in the Colonial Era*. Newport News, VA: Mariners' Museum, 1953.

National Register of Historic Places Registration Form. Virginia Department of Historic Resources, Richmond, VA: 1999.

O'Hara, Lucy Hudgins. *Yorktown, As I Remember*. Verona, VA: McClure Printing, 1981.

Quarstein, John V., and J. Michael Moore. *Yorktown's Civil War Siege—Drums Along the Warwick*. Charleston, SC: The History Press, 2012.

Richmond Compiler, October 1881.

Richmond Daily Dispatch, October 22, 1881.

Richmond Enquirer, October 1881.

Richmond Examiner, October, 1881.

Rowland, Kate Mason. "The Virginia Cavaliers." *The Southern Bivouac* 1, no. 11 (April 1886).

Sands, John O. *Yorktown's Captive Fleet*. Charlottesville: University of Virginia Press, 1983.

Sears, Stephen W. *To the Gates of Richmond: The Peninsula Campaign*. New York: Ticknor & Fields, 1992.

Sinclair, Caroline Baytop. *Gloucester's Past in Pictures*. Virginia Beach, VA: Donning Company, 1991.

Smith, Margaret P. *Old Yorktown and Its History*. Yorktown, VA: Mrs. Sydney Smith, 1920.

Sweet, Julia Ann. "Virginia Celebrates the Yorktown Centennial of 1881." Master's thesis, University of Richmond, 1996.

Taylor, L.B., Jr. *The Ghosts of Williamsburg*. Vol. 2. Williamsburg, VA: L.B. Taylor, 1999.

INDEX

ABOUT THE AUTHOR

Historian Wilford Kale is a retired newspaperman and Virginia state agency official who has been involved with researching and writing history for much of his adult life. An alumnus of the College of William and Mary, he received his bachelor's degree in history from Park College (now Park University) and his master of philosophy degree in history from the University of Leicester, Leicester, England. His most recent books include *From Student to Warrior—A Military History of the College of William and Mary* and *A Very Virginia Christmas—Stories & Traditions.*

Visit us at
www.historypress.com
···